This book is such a helpful tool for meditation on the Word of God. Out of such meditation comes a true knowledge of the Living God. John 1:1-4. Intercession can then spring forth from the very heart of God. The Lord's Prayer in Luke 11:2-4 gives us the true focus of all prayer. That focus is to see His Kingdom manifest on earth even as it is in Heaven. Only God's power can change things and bring Heaven's rule to earth, but the meditating, receiving, and praying to see this happen has been given to us.

I believe one of the greatest things about this devotional is the fact that it came forth not only by revelation but by obedience. Susan was given at least two prophetic words that she was to write books. It caught her by surprise. She did not see writing as a call on her life at that time. However, she prayed, meditated on God's Word and believed the Word of the Lord through the Prophets. She then began the process. As time passed and more revelation came, she became more convinced and more excited about this portion of anointing given her by the Spirit of God. This is just the tip of the iceberg, and the beginning of a journey that will, not only bless her life, but countless others.

It is a wonderful example of hearing the voice of God and then going forth in faith. It is also such a great example of using what God has put in one's hand. It was in her hand but she had not been made aware until the word came through the Prophets. 2 Chronicles 20:20 says "Believe the Lord your God and you shall be established. Believe His Prophets and you shall prosper".

I believe great blessings are in store for those who read and participate in this encouragement in meditation and that a rich legacy will be left for others through Susan's writings now and in the future.

Erma Stogsdill, Shekinah Free Indeed Ministries

I am so proud to know and serve with Susan Schrader. Her calling and faithfulness to the ministry of prayer is inspirational. In a time when this generation needs to recapture the essence and power of prayer, Susan has written a prayer devotional that is simple and easy to follow but also scripturally sound. This book will be rich and rewarding to the careful reader.

May God bless this book and help us to focus our lives on one of God's primary passions, prayer.

Joe Skiles, Senior Pastor Solid Rock Church

This is an outstanding devotional! Susan is a passionate intercessor who loves God and has a vision to see people's lives changed as they encounter Him. This devotional offers so much wisdom and encouragement to live the life God has created us all to live. You will be blessed and know that GOD loves you and desires you to live a life of freedom in Him!"

Crystal Jennings, Prayer Ministry Director of Solid Rock Church

❖ACKNOWLEDGEMENTS❖

THANKS TO…

Jesus Christ, for putting this book on my heart and allowing me to be His vessel to work through. For His wisdom and revelation He has given in this book.

My husband, for his love and support while writing this book and for helping me with the final preparation to get it printed.

Erma, Crystal, and Pastor Skiles for their endorsements and support. I appreciate their influence on my life.

Christian Photo Shops. www.christianphotoshops.com

MEDITATE ON GOD'S WORD: PRAYER

Daily Devotions to
Help Become an
Excellent Intercessor

Susan Patricia Schrader

Resources:

❖ INTRODUCTION ❖
❧❧❧❧❧❧❧❧❧❧❧❧

This is a different kind of devotional than most people are used to. The Lord desires for His children to get into the Word more and meditate on it. Meditate means to reflect; to moan, to mutter; to ponder; to make a quiet sound such as sighing; to meditate or contemplate something as one repeats the words.

Reflect and ponder the Scriptures until you have them down in your spirit. It isn't necessarily memorizing the verse but reflecting on it and asking the Lord for the revelation of it.

You will have success in your life if you meditate on the Word day and night. You must get the Word in your spirit rather than just in your mind if you want to receive insight and revelation from the Lord.

How can a person meditate day and night? The same way we are to pray continually. By being constantly in a state of communion and fellowship with God and reflecting on the Word rather than reading just to be reading. It is good to just read the Word but it is better to take a portion of Scripture and meditate on it until you understand it and receive insight and revelation of it.

In this devotion, I am taking portions of Scripture a week for 52 weeks regarding prayer and meditating on that portion all week. After each day, I give a prayer or declaration on that Scripture. These are to just get you started with your prayers. At the end of the week, I give a summary of that Scripture. You can go on and study it further or go on to the next week's portion of Scripture. I recommend you only do the daily devotion which is short and reflect and meditate on it rather than complete the whole week in one day.

It is important to get into a routine of meditating on the Word of God. I only gave the reference of the verses I'm using because you need to look up these verses and read them from your Bible rather than just reading them from this book. I may not talk about the whole portion of Scripture I have given but it is important to read the whole context around it.

The first few weeks I am presenting Scriptures about the importance of the Word of God and meditating on it. Then I will present Scriptures regarding prayer. This devotion doesn't give a formula for prayer or steps on how to pray but I am just giving different Scriptures that talk about prayer that are good to meditate on and will help you with prayer and hopefully answer some questions about prayer.

I have written these devotions from Jesus' point of view; i.e., the first person singular (I, Me, Mine) always refers to Christ or Father God. "You" refers to you, the reader, so the idea is that of Jesus speaking to you.

❧❧❧❧❧❧❧❧❧❧❧❧❧❧❧❧❧❧❧❧❧❧❧❧❧

WEEK 1
❖MEDITATE ON GOD'S WORD❖

❧❧❧❧❧❧❧❧❧❧❧❧❧❧❧❧❧❧❧❧❧❧❧❧❧

DAY 1
Read Joshua 1:1-9; Psalm 1:1-3

The first step in learning to possess your inheritance in Me is to know My Word. This Scripture shows that this involves studying My Word and thinking about it so that it will become a complete part of the way you live.

Memorize, ponder, and speak Scripture regularly. Intentionally apply My Word to your life; it will produce great success. Be like a sponge and soak in My Word. Soak it up and then you can wring it out on others.

Thank You, Father, for Your Word. Help me to study Your Word diligently and think on it continually. I declare I will meditate on Your Word continually. In Jesus' name Amen.

❧❧❧❧❧❧❧❧❧❧❧

DAY 2
Read Joshua 1:1-9; Psalm 1:1-3

What do I mean by meditate on My Word? To meditate upon My Word is to reflect, ponder, and quietly repeat them in soft continuous sound while utterly abandoning outside distractions.

I will give an example of a cat stalking a squirrel. It slinks real slow, focused completely on the squirrel not letting anything distract her. As she gets closer she pounces on the squirrel.

That is what I want you to do as you meditate on My Word. Stay completely focused, no distractions go slowly and suddenly you'll have the revelation. The cat may miss the squirrel but you will receive the revelation.

Father, help me to stay focused on Your Word and not let distractions interfere and that I go slowly as I read Your Word. Thank You Lord. In Jesus' name Amen.

DAY 3
Read Joshua 1:1-9; Psalm 1:1-3

My Word shall not depart out of your mouth which means to continually speak My Word and pray My Word.

You are to declare and decree My Word. To speak, confess and declare My Word you have to know the Word, by reading and meditating on My Word. To pray effectively, you need to do these things. Your words are important; watch what you say.

Thank You, Father, for Your Word. I will speak it, confess it, and meditate on it. In Jesus' name Amen.

DAY 4
Read Joshua 1:1-9; Psalm 1:1-3

You are to meditate on My Word day and night. You are probably thinking how can I meditate on the Word day and night? Memorize My Word; go over it as many times as you can, do this 52 week devotion. Pick an area you are dealing with, find passages dealing with that issue and take a verse a week, daily go over it, praying for revelation of that verse and eventually it will get down in your spirit.

It's good to memorize Scripture but if you get the revelation of it, you'll remember it better. That's what this devotion is all about, 52 weeks of Scriptures to become an expert intercessor. This can be done with any issue or topic.

Father, I declare I will study Your Word and meditate on it day and night and get revelation from You regarding the Scripture I am studying. In Jesus' name Amen.

DAY 5
Read Joshua 1:1-9; Psalm 1:1-3

If you will observe and do all that is written in My Word, you shall make your way prosperous, and do wisely and have good success. It is not Me making you prosperous and successful. You can make your way prosperous, deal wisely and have good success if you meditate on My Word day and night.

You aren't to sit around waiting for Me to make you prosperous and successful. It is your responsibility and you do it by meditating on My Word continually.

There are many, many riches in My Word that you have to dig for. Treasure found nowhere else. The Bible (My Word) is so very important for victory in your life. Make it a priority in your life.

Father, I declare I will meditate on Your Word day and night and make myself prosperous and successful and be wise. I thank You, Lord, for Your Word. In Jesus name Amen.

DAY 6
Read Joshua 1:1-9; Psalm 1:1-3

It says in Psalm 1 verse 2 that you are to delight in My Word and meditate on it day and night. If you do, verse 3 says you will be like a tree firmly planted by streams of water, ready to bring forth its fruit in its season and its leaf will never fade or wither; and everything you do shall prosper and come to maturity.

To prosper and mature in Me, you must find time to meditate on My Word. Make it a priority in your life. Meditating on My Word is the only way you will mature and learn of Me and bear fruit. You must know My Word. It is your instruction manual for life and your prayer guide.

Thank You, Father, for Your Word. I declare I will study and meditate on the Word of God and bear fruit. In Jesus' name Amen.

DAY 7 - SUMMARY
Read Joshua 1:1-9; Psalm 1:1-3

These verses are telling you if you meditate, ponder, mutter, reflect on My Word you will be prosperous, successful and wise. You must get My Word down in your heart for it to be effective. Just reading My Word, skimming over it won't help; you must meditate on it day and night.

Take a verse for a week, study it, and meditate over it, repeating it and you'll receive My revelation. Do this for any issue you are dealing with and you will come to maturity and be fruitful.

Father, I declare I will study and meditate on Your Word day and night so that I will be prosperous, successful, wise, and fruitful and be mature in Christ. In Jesus' name Amen.

NOTES:

෧෧෧෧෧෧෧෧෧෧෧෧෧෧෧෧෧෧෧෧෧෧෧෧෧෧

WEEK 2
❖INSPIRED WORD OF GOD❖

෧෧෧෧෧෧෧෧෧෧෧෧෧෧෧෧෧෧෧෧෧෧෧෧෧෧

DAY 1
Read 2 Timothy 3:16-17; 2 Peter 1:20-21

I breathed every Scripture in My Word. The Scripture is the product of My creative breath. This is why you hear it called "The Word of God" because it is My living voice.

This doesn't mean the writers were like robots seized upon by My power to write automatically without their conscious participation. I do not override gifts of intellect and sensitivity that I have given My people. The writers have surrendered their will to the leading of My Holy Spirit.

Father, I declare that I revere Your Word and recognize it's fully divine source of inspiration and submit to it. In Jesus' name Amen.

DAY 2
Read 2 Timothy 3:16-17; 2 Peter 1:20-21

My Word is profitable for instruction. My Word will give you instruction, teaching, training for what you need for any situation you may have. My Word is your instruction manual and prayer guide. I know a lot of people don't like to read instructions when putting something together because they think they know how to do it and don't want to take the time to read it but 99% of the time, it gets messed up.

That is the same way with My Word. You may think you can handle life without reading the instruction manual but things would go so much better if you would read what I have to say about it.

Father, thank You for the instructions, teaching and training that You give me from Your Word. I declare I will read and meditate on it day and night. In Jesus' name Amen.

DAY 3
Read 2 Timothy 3:16-17; 2 Peter 1:20-21

My Word is profitable for reproof or to show you what is wrong in your life. My Word will convict you of sin. As you read My Word and it convicts you, just repent and I will forgive you and show you in My Word how to overcome that sin. I love you and want to set you free from all bondages and problems in your life.

Father, I declare I will read Your Word and allow it to show me where I am living wrong so I can repent and be free. In Jesus' name Amen.

DAY 4
Read 2 Timothy 3:16-17; 2 Peter 1:20-21

My Word is for correction of error and discipline in obedience. My Word will show you where you are in error of your beliefs or your thoughts. My thoughts and ways are higher than yours.
My Word will show you how to walk in obedience to My will and Word. To receive My blessings, you must walk in obedience to My Word.

Father, I declare Your Word shows me where I have gotten into error of what I think or believe and it shows me how to obey You and walk in Your will. In Jesus' name Amen.

❧❧❧❧❧❧❧❧❧❧❧

DAY 5
Read 2 Timothy 3:16-17; 2 Peter 1:20-21

My Word is also for training in righteousness. You are righteous because of My blood shed on the cross but My Word will show you how to live holy lives and how to conform to My will in your thoughts, purpose and actions. You are to be a living sacrifice and are not to conform to this world (Romans 12:1-2).

Father, I declare I am receiving from Your Word how to live holy and how to conform to Your will in my thoughts, purpose and actions. I am a living sacrifice for You and I do not conform to this world. In Jesus' name Amen.

DAY 6
Read 2 Timothy 3:16-17; 2 Peter 1:20-21

I breathed every Scripture in the Bible and it is profitable for everyday living. You can be complete and proficient and well fitted, thoroughly equipped for every good work by reading and meditating on My Word. My Word will equip you and help you be proficient for every good work (2 Tim 2:21).

Father, I declare I am complete and proficient, well fitted and equipped as I meditate on Your Word for every good work You call me to do. In Jesus' name Amen.

DAY 7 - SUMMARY
Read 2 Timothy 3:16-17; 2 Peter 1:20-21

I breathed every Word in Scripture and it is profitable to instruct you, to convict you of your sins, correct your wrong thinking and help you be obedient to My will and train you in holy living in conformity to My will.

I want to stress that I am not going to put sickness on you to teach you something. I've heard people say that and that is not truth. You may learn something from it and I will work things out for your good if you are My child but if you would get into My Word, I will teach you through My Word rather than sickness or hard knocks or some terrible trial you are going through.

You have to take responsibility for your part in things happening in your life. I am always speaking and you will hear from Me much better if you are in My Word studying and meditating on it. Remember, My Word is your instruction manual for everyday and every situation.

Thank You, Father, for the divine inspired Word of God that you have given to me to help me in my everyday walk with You. In Jesus' name Amen.

NOTES:

ʒʒʒʒʒʒʒʒʒʒʒʒʒʒʒʒʒʒʒʒ

WEEK 3
❖VALUE OF GOD'S WORD❖

ʒʒʒʒʒʒʒʒʒʒʒʒʒʒʒʒʒʒʒʒ

DAY 1
Read Psalm 19:7-11

My Word is perfect, it restores the whole person, it rejoices the heart, and it is pure and bright, enlightening the eyes. My Word is true and righteous, sweeter than honey and keeping My Word brings great reward. My truth will prevail because I am truth.

Father, I declare Your Word is of great value. It is perfect; it restores me, and rejoices my heart. It enlightens my eyes because it is true and righteous and brings me great reward. In Jesus' name Amen.

DAY 2
Read Psalm 19:7-11

My Word is perfect, accurate, and exact, entirely without flaws, defects or shortcomings. It is correct in every detail.

I am perfect and a good, good Father. You can trust My Word and My promises.

Father, I declare Your law is perfect, without flaws and correct in every detail. I love You and Your Word. In Jesus' name Amen.

DAY 3
Read Psalm 19:7-11

My Word restores the whole person. Do you need restored? My Word is a living seed and as you read and meditate on it, it brings life and restoration to you. It gives understanding to you and direction for your life. Get in My Word and stay in My Word and you will be restored.

Father, I declare Your Word restores me and I can understand Your Word because Your Spirit dwells within me giving me the insight and revelation. In Jesus' name Amen.

DAY 4
Read Psalm 19:7-11

My Word rejoices the heart. Are you down in the dumps? My joy is your strength. Read My Word and it will put joy and strength in your heart and will enlighten your eyes. It gives light to direct your path. It is a lamp to your feet and a light to your path (Psalm 119:105).

A lamp will only light up a little bit, even a flashlight will only light up a little ways so you have to trust Me to direct your path and stay where the light is shining.

Father, Your Word gives me joy and enlightens my eyes so that I have understanding and You shine light on my path to direct me. In Jesus' name Amen.

DAY 5
Read Psalm 19:7-11

My Word is to be desired more than gold or silver. If you knew there was a million dollars buried in your backyard, would you dig up your yard any way you could to find that million dollars? Maybe you would get a bulldozer or whatever big machine to dig the yard up. You probably wouldn't use just a shovel. You wouldn't get very far, very fast. I think you would do whatever it would take to find that million dollars. Are you digging as diligently for those treasures I have placed in My Word as you would for that million dollars?

Place great value on My Word. It exceeds all earth's values. My Word is a treasure beyond compare. The believer finds in My Word wealth beyond this world, sweeter than honey, more costly than gold, and to be desired above all else. My Word will transform, heal, and lead you into a deeper relationship with Me, your loving Father.

Father, I praise and worship You. I thank You for Your Word that You have given to me. Help me to value it more than worldly wealth because You have given me treasures in Your Word and I need to be digging for those treasures. Your Word is better than diamonds and sweeter than honey or any amount of worldly wealth. In Jesus' name Amen.

DAY 6
Read Psalm 19:7-11

Through My Word, I warn of danger and show how to get out of danger. When you keep My Word and meditate on it, there is great reward. What is this great reward? All the things we discussed so far and so much more that you can find in My Word. It is a gold mine of hidden treasure. Happy hunting!

Father, I declare I will meditate on Your Word and receive warnings as well as instruction how to get out of danger and find great rewards and treasures. In Jesus' name Amen.

DAY 7 - SUMMARY
Read Psalm 19:7-11

There are many, many more Scriptures that talk about the value of My Word. The whole chapter of Psalm 119 talks about the importance of My Word. Take time to read it and meditate on it.

In the portion that we studied this week I am saying that My Word will restore the whole person, give understanding to the simple, enlighten the eyes, they are true and righteous and are to be desired more than gold. My Word is full of hidden treasure that you must dig for but you will receive great reward by doing so.

Father, I declare Your Word is of great value and I will dig into it to receive all that You desire to give me through the study and meditation of Your Word. I love You and Your Word. In Jesus' name Amen.

NOTES:

෯෯෯෯෯෯෯෯෯෯෯෯෯෯෯෯෯෯෯෯෯෯

WEEK 4
❖ATTEND TO GOD'S WORD❖

෯෯෯෯෯෯෯෯෯෯෯෯෯෯෯෯෯෯෯෯෯෯

DAY 1
Read Proverbs 4:1-10, 20-24

Attend to my words would mean to pay attention to or listen to My Word. Read or listen to My Word. Listen to teachings of My Word. You are to submit to these sayings. Surrender to these words and let them not depart from your sight.

You are to meditate on My Word, keep them before you continuously to get them and keep them in the center of your heart.

Father, I declare I will pay attention and listen to Your Words and submit to them. I will meditate on Your Word and get them in the center of my heart. In Jesus' name Amen.

෯෯෯෯෯෯෯෯෯෯෯

DAY 2
Read Proverbs 4:1-10, 20-24

Pay attention to My Word in order to gain and to know intelligent discernment, comprehension, and interpretation of spiritual matters (Proverbs 4:1). That sounds like a good reason to pay attention to My Word.

I want to give you intelligent discernment. Could you use intelligent discernment? That would mean more of an understanding of spiritual things in My Word. You gain it by paying attention to My Word.

Father, I desire intelligent discernment and more understanding of You and Your Word. I declare I will give attention to Your Word to receive that discernment. In Jesus' name Amen.

DAY 3
Read Proverbs 4:1-10, 20-24

Do you want to gain comprehension which is the ability to know and understand My Word and gain interpretation of My Word and spiritual matters? I will give you the interpretation of My Word and of spiritual matters if you pay attention and submit to My sayings and be obedient to My Word.

Father, I declare I will attend to Your Word and gain understanding and interpretation of Your Word and of spiritual matters. In Jesus' name Amen.

DAY 4
Read Proverbs 4:1-10, 20-24

If you attend and submit to My Word it will be life to you, healing and health to all your flesh. Do you need healing and health and abundant life? Then get into My Word, meditate on it until it is in the center of your heart and you will receive life and health. I am the Word and I give you life abundantly (John 10:10).

Father, I declare I have life abundantly and healing in my flesh because I attend to Your Word and it is in the center of my heart. In Jesus' name Amen.

∞∞∞∞∞∞∞∞∞∞∞

DAY 5
Read Proverbs 4:1-10, 20-24

 Keep and guard your heart with all vigilance for it affects everything you do. This means to guard and be watchful to what you hear, see, watch on TV, read, and say because what goes in your heart will come out of your mouth.

 For out of the fullness of your heart your mouth speaks (Matthew 12:34). You need to put good things in your heart by reading and meditating on My Word. Be watchful.

Father, I declare I am watchful of the things I put before my eyes, the things I watch on TV, the things I read and the things I hear. I declare I will put the Word before me and allow only the Word in my heart so that is what flows out of my mouth. In Jesus' name Amen.

∞∞∞∞∞∞∞∞∞∞∞

DAY 6
Read Proverbs 4:1-10, 20-24

 Put away from you false and dishonest speech and contrary talk. Watch what you say and how you say things. You need to speak positive things and speak good things to others. Speak encouraging words to others and to yourself. Speak My Word over others and yourself.

 Don't put people down or speak falsely to them. Sometimes your jokes put people down even if you don't mean it. Speak the truth. Speak the Word and I will bless you.

Father, I declare I will not speak falsely or dishonest things or contrary things. I will watch what I say to myself and to others. In Jesus' name Amen.

DAY 7 - SUMMARY
Read Proverbs 4:1-10, 20-24

You are to attend to My Word and submit to My sayings. Let My Word not depart from your sight and get them in the center of your heart. When you do, you will have life and health to all your flesh.

Keep and guard your heart and watch what you hear and say because what you put in your heart will come out. Your character will be known by what comes out of your heart and out of your mouth.

If you listen to cussing all the time, that is what will be in your heart and what will come out of your mouth. If you read and listen to My Word, that is what will be in your heart and what will come out of your mouth. Be watchful and attend to My Word and you will have life and health to all your flesh.

Thank You, Father, for Your Word that gives me life and health. I declare I will meditate on it and get it in the center of my heart so that I can live and talk by Your Word. In Jesus' name Amen.

NOTES:

WEEK 5
❖GOD'S SPIRIT RESTS ON YOU❖

DAY 1
Read Isaiah 11:1-5

My anointing will be on you, will rest on you, settle, comfort, and be placed on you just as it was on Me. The Spirit of the Lord refers to My breath and My touch on you. As you realize this, your praying will be more effective.

My Spirit will enable you to have wisdom, understanding, counsel, power, knowledge and to reverently fear Me. I have consecrated or anointed you and furnished what is needed.

Father, thank You that Your anointing rests upon me just as it did on Jesus and that Your Spirit enables me to have wisdom, understanding, counsel, power, knowledge and the fear of the Lord and that I am consecrated through You. In Jesus' name Amen.

DAY 2
Read Isaiah 11:1-5

My Spirit gives you Godly wisdom and understanding. My wisdom is principles of right living put into practice. Seek My wisdom above all else. My wisdom will also give you insight and enlightenment into the true nature of things.

I will give you understanding to intelligently assess a situation and analyze and discern situations. Ask Me for wisdom and I will liberally give it to you (James 1:5-6).

Father, give me Godly wisdom and understanding of who You are. I seek wisdom above all else. I want to have the understanding of intelligently assessing a situation and discerning the things of Your Kingdom. In Jesus' name Amen.

DAY 3
Read Isaiah 11:1-5

My Spirit will counsel, advise and admonish you and give you power, strength and ability to do all I call you to.

I will give you knowledge which is the ability to perceive, understand, know, discern, to be aware of, insight and intelligence of all things. Knowledge of Me along with reverently fearing Me describes the proper relationship between Me and those who truly obey Me.

If you truly recognize Me as all powerful, this will be reflected in your attitude and daily life in the form of reverence. To understand Me is to delight in Me as delighting in a sweet fragrance. Do you enjoy smelling sweet smelling flowers in a garden? How does it make you feel? As you delight in smelling the roses, delight in Me.

Father, I want to delight in the fear of the Lord as I delight in a sweet smell. Teach me to delight in You this way. In Jesus' name Amen.

DAY 4
Read Isaiah 11:1-5

My Spirit is resting on you enabling you to do these things that I was enabled to do through the Spirit.

My Spirit will be a comfort to you as My touch comes on you. You have been touched by My very hand. I am always there for you.

Jesus, reveal the deep truth of this to me that I can realize the significance of this and how it can apply when I am praying for others. The touch of the Lord settled and placed on me with wisdom, discernment, understanding, counsel, power, knowledge and reverential fear of the Lord. WOW! Thank You Lord. In Jesus' name Amen

DAY 5
Read Isaiah 11:1-5

My Spirit will rest on you and will also be in you. You are the temple of My Holy Spirit where He dwells. My Spirit resides in you (1 Corinthians.6:19). Actually, your whole being is surrounded by My Spirit because My Spirit is residing in you and settled upon you.

My Spirit is in you and on you. How can you fail as you pray with so much of the Spirit on you and in you? You need to not think as you pray but allow My Spirit to pray through you as My Spirit gives you wisdom, understanding, counsel, power, knowledge, discernment, and reverence for Me.

Father, renew my mind to focus on the Spirit and the words will come from the Spirit what's needed to be prayed. It will flow freely. Thank You Lord. In Jesus' name Amen.

DAY 6
Read Isaiah 11:1-5

What do I mean when I mention the fear of the Lord in these verses? To fear Me means to reverence Me, not be fearful of Me but to be in awe of Me and delight in that reverence as delighting in a sweet smell.

When you smell something sweet, it can affect your whole being; especially if you take a deep breath, smell deeply. You lavish in it. It makes you feel good. You delight in it. That is the way I want you to delight in Me. I want to delight your senses.

Father, I stand in awe of You and I am consumed by Your awesome presence and the sweet fragrance of Your presence overwhelms me. I thank You Father for loving me so much and sending Jesus to die for me. In Jesus' name Amen.

DAY 7 - SUMMARY
Read Isaiah 11:1-5

My breath, My Spirit, My anointing settles on you and is in you to enable you with principles of living, intelligently assessing a situation, to admonish, to be empowered by My Spirit and have a reverence for Me and delight in Me as delighting in a sweet smell.

These verses were originally speaking about Me but since My Spirit dwells within you, the Scripture also refers to you and enables you to do and have what I have and do what I could do. By My anointing, as intercessors you are empowered to pray prayers that are led by My Spirit.

Father, I declare that the Spirit of the Lord anoints me and enables me to do all that Jesus was enabled to do. I can be a powerful intercessor because the Spirit of the Lord is upon me and in me directing me, helping me to intercede as the Spirit leads. In Jesus 'name Amen.

NOTES:

≈≈≈≈≈≈≈≈≈≈≈≈≈≈≈≈≈≈≈≈≈≈≈≈

WEEK 6
❖ASK IN JESUS' NAME❖

≈≈≈≈≈≈≈≈≈≈≈≈≈≈≈≈≈≈≈≈≈≈≈≈

DAY 1
Read John 14:1-14

I know it is hard for you to imagine doing greater things than I did but as you allow My Spirit to work in and through you, you can do these things. You also must believe in Me as Savior to do these greater works. You cannot do them on your own.

You will not necessarily do more significant things than I did but you are expected to heal the sick, raise the dead, cast out demons, speak in new tongues, etc. By My Spirit you can do these things. You are able to go further and you have internet and TV now which I did not have, which expands My message to reach everyone.

Father, I declare that I will do the things that Jesus did and even greater things than these as I allow the Holy Spirit to lead me to do the works. In Jesus' name Amen.

DAY 2
Read John 14:1-14

I am telling you in these verses to ask in My name when you pray. As Intercessors, you are to be insistent but not commanding, without any qualms because I give you the authority in My name to ask as My representatives.

Acting as My representative means that the person calling on My name is in a close relationship with Me and wants what I want and wants to glorify our Father.

Father, I declare that I will ask in Jesus' name because You give me the authority to ask in His name and You will do it as long as I ask in accordance to Your will and You will be glorified. In Jesus' name Amen.

DAY 3
Read John 14:1-14

Our Father has given you My name to use with authority. Don't be afraid to use My name. You can use it to heal the sick, rebuke the Devil, deliver the oppressed.

Without My name, your prayers are useless. In My name, you can ask and receive to glorify our Father.

Thank You, Father, for giving me authority in Jesus' name to outwit the Devil, to heal the sick and deliver the oppressed. I declare I can be victorious in every area of my life by having the revelation of the authority God gives me and pray for others with that authority and set the captives free. In Jesus' name Amen.

DAY 4
Read John 14:1-14

You can ask and pray in confidence because I hear you and will answer you. In My name, you can boldly come into our Father's presence.

When interceding for others, ask in confidence knowing that you will receive what you ask for in My name. You must ask in My name.

Father, I declare that I ask in confidence because I believe and have faith knowing You hear me and will answer me as I pray. In Jesus' name Amen.

DAY 5
Read John 14:1-14

Imitate Me, doing and being like Me, even doing greater things than I have done. I will give you the ability if you are willing vessels. Everything you do is to glorify our Father.

Everything you ask is to glorify our Father. If you are asking something that will not glorify our Father, it will not get answered. You must ask in My name, in faith and with the right motive to receive an answer to prayer.

Father, I declare that I will glorify You, Jesus in all that I do. Help me, change me to be as powerful and effective as You, Lord, in what I do for the Kingdom. In Jesus' name Amen.

DAY 6
Read John 14:1-14

You have to ask with confidence but also with the right motives for Me to answer your prayers, not ask for selfish desires but things that glorify our Father and increase His Kingdom.

You are My representative on the earth to proclaim the message and further My Kingdom.

Father, I will ask in confidence and with the right motives to glorify You and the Kingdom. In Jesus' name Amen.

DAY 7 - SUMMARY
Read John 14:1-14

You are to do even greater things on this earth than I did. I have given you My power and authority to overcome evil. You are to ask for anything in My name and I will give it to you if it will glorify our Father.

You must imitate Me and walk as I walked on the earth. Study My Word and My life so that you can imitate Me and do the things that I did because in My name you are able to do it.

My Spirit will empower you because I dwell within you waiting on you to be My representative and intercessor on the earth. As you allow Me to, I will flow through you to accomplish My will on the earth.

Father, thank You for empowering me to do all that Jesus did while on the earth. As I study the Word, show me the things Jesus did and how He walked in faith to do Your will. In Jesus' name Amen.

NOTES:

WEEK 7
❖FOCUS ON THINGS ABOVE❖

DAY 1
Read Colossians 3:1-4; Joshua 1:8

You identify with Me since you have been raised with Me, the old life and thinking is crucified. This is speaking of your spirit, not your body. Before you accept Me, your spirit is dead to Me, after accepting Me your spirit becomes alive to Me and brand new. I am now living in you.

You are to set your hearts and minds on things above, not on earthly things. As you meditate on things above, where I am seated at the right hand of our Father, your thinking will be as I think.

Father, I declare when Christ was raised from the dead, I was raised with Him and have become a new creation. Thank You that the old is gone and the new has come. I declare I am a new creation in Christ. In Jesus' name Amen.

આઆઆઆઆઆઆઆઆઆઆ

DAY 2
Read Colossians 3:1-4: Joshua 1:8

You are to seek those things which are above. You are to seek first My kingdom and My righteousness and all the things you need shall be added to you (Matthew 6:33). You are to acknowledge Me in all your ways, and I will direct your path (Proverbs 3:6).

Be fully of Me and in fellowship with Me. You need to get to that place of total surrender to Me, surrendering your thoughts, ideas, and plans at My feet and let Me take over. You need to seek Me first in all things and I will direct your path.

Father, forgive me for not always seeking those things which are above and acknowledging You in all things. I declare I will acknowledge You in all things and You will direct my path. In Jesus' name Amen.

DAY 3
Read Colossians 3:1-4: Joshua 1:8

You are to crucify the flesh and be raised with Me. Set your hearts on things above. You either have your heart on the things of the world or on things above where I am seated at the right hand of God our Father. What is in your heart will eventually come out. If your heart is set on Me and My Word you'll be able to flow with My Spirit.

You can really get bogged down looking at the things on the earth. Don't let circumstances and situations in the world trip you up. Keep focused on Me and My Word and never forget that I am with you always. My Spirit dwells within you so you have nothing to fear in this world. You will have victory in your life if you set your mind on things above.

Father, I declare that the Spirit flows from my heart because I have crucified the flesh and I am allowing the Spirit to lead me and pray through me. I set my mind on things above, not on the earth. I have victory in Jesus Christ. In Jesus' name Amen.

DAY 4
Read Colossians 3:1-4: Joshua 1:8

When you accept Me, you died to this earthly realm and now live hidden in Me. Hidden in Me is being in the Secret Place (Psalm 91:1) As the bird protects it's young under its wing, I will protect you from the elements of the world. Nothing can get to the young as long as it stays under her wing.

I will keep sickness and disease from you. It will not come near you as long as you trust Me. The devil will try to put symptoms on you. Don't give in to those symptoms. Just as the little bird may be swayed from its mother's protective wings, as long as the young stays under her wings, it will be protected. Don't let temptation sway you from the Secret Place. The worldly things are desirous but I will give you all you need and desire and will protect you. Trust Me and keep your eyes, mind, thoughts, and life focused on Me and My Word and I will continue to give you revelation of My Word.

Father, I declare I am hidden in You (in the Secret Place) protected from the world as I keep my mind set on You. In Jesus' name Amen.

⁋⁋⁋⁋⁋⁋⁋⁋⁋⁋⁋

DAY 5
Read Colossians 3:1-4: Joshua 1:8

When I appear, you will be with Me and will share in all My glory. Your life is in Me. So you live in this earthly body by trusting in Me, I love you and gave Myself for you. You are no longer slaves to sin (Romans 6:6). You are more than conquerors through Me (Romans 8:37). For in Me you live and move and exist (Acts 17:28).

Father, I declare my life is in You. I am dead to sin. I live and move and exist in You alone. Thank You, Jesus. In Jesus' name Amen.

DAY 6
Read Colossians 3:1-4: Joshua 1:8

I will keep you in perfect peace, when your mind is stayed on Me and when you trust in Me. I will help you pray with others as you keep your mind on Me. Pray what you want to be prayed for. Put yourself in the other persons place. Have compassion and passion for them.

Feel with them what they are feeling. Look into their eyes; check their facial expressions. Be sensitive to My Spirit and flow with Me. I will love them through you as you allow Me to.

Father, I declare I will keep my mind on You and trust You completely so I will have perfect peace. I will have compassion on those I pray for. Thank You Lord. In Jesus' name Amen.

DAY 7 – SUMMARY
Read Colossians 3:1-4: Joshua 1:8

You are to keep your mind set on heavenly things not on earthly things. Be involved with Christians, go to church and meditate day and night on My Word. I love you and the Spirit dwells in you to help you to stay focused on Me and My Word.

As intercessors you have to set your mind on things above to allow My Spirit to flow through you. I can't flow through you to pray effective powerful prayers if you have your mind set on the things of earth.

Thank You, Father, for this verse that tells me to set my mind on heavenly things. Since You tell me to do this, it is not impossible because You don't tell me anything to do that You will not help me to do. Nothing is impossible with You. I love You and praise Your Holy name. In Jesus' name Amen.

NOTES:

WEEK 8
❖BE MOVED BY COMPASSION❖

DAY 1
Read Matthew 9:35-38

When I saw the crowds, I had compassion on them because they were harassed and helpless, like sheep without a shepherd. I was moved with deep compassion, pity, sympathy and I dealt gently with them.

What motivates you to pray? My love needs to be your motivator; otherwise, you'll just go through the motions and not be sincere with what you say in your prayers.

Your prayers need to be heartfelt prayers which mean you are to yield yourself to Me and just pray from your heart. If it's not in your heart to cry or pray a certain way or say a certain thing, don't fake it. Don't work it up. Be sincere in what you are praying.

My love will cause you to be moved with compassion. When you have compassion, you don't just pity someone who is in trouble; you suffer with them. Compassion draws you so that you hurt because someone else hurts.

I declare the compassion of the Lord flows from me to others as I pray for them. When I see someone hurting, I will have compassion on them and minister to them. In Jesus' name Amen.

DAY 2
Read Matthew 9:35-38

My Spirit dwells within you so you have My compassion dwelling within you but you need to release it. You have everything about Me in you and My Spirit wants to release it out to others.

My compassion also means I have mercy and tenderly love those in need. Mercy is an active desire to remove the cause of distress in others. Mercy and compassion go together.

Lord, as I intercede for others, help me to have mercy and compassion, hurt with them and let the Spirit flow through me to pray effectively. In Jesus' name Amen.

DAY 3
Read Matthew 9:35-38

Truest compassion is only found in My nature, because only I know the full depth of an individual's pain, need, or suffering. I have seen and feel human weaknesses (Hebrews 4:15), fully sensing the ravaged condition of human brokenness.

To grow in My love, pray to experience it. You need to identify with those in need. Make their needs your own as you pray, especially those that are lost.

Father, I want to be like Jesus and have His heart of compassion. How can I pray for anyone without having the love and compassion of Jesus? I don't think it is possible. I declare I release out of my spirit to those lost and hurting. In Jesus' name Amen.

DAY 4
Read Matthew 9:35-38

Sheep are stupid animals because they can't do anything for themselves; they have to have a shepherd. My Word likens you to sheep because you also need a shepherd. You think you're smart enough to make it on your own but you're not. You need Me as your Shepherd.

I will take care of you as a shepherd takes care of his sheep. The sheep put total trust in the shepherd because they have to depend on him to survive.

You need to see lost, hurting, and helpless people as sheep without a shepherd, needing Me, their good Shepherd to come and gather them into My arms and take care of them. You need to show mercy and compassion.

Father, like sheep I need a shepherd who tends, leads, guides, cherishes, feeds, and protects a flock. Jesus is my good Shepherd and I need to pray for those that are lost and helpless find Jesus. In Jesus' name Amen.

DAY 5
Read Matthew 9:35-38

The people in these Scriptures were dispirited and distressed, like sheep without a shepherd. My people are referred to as sheep in Scripture. You are My sheep and I am your Shepherd (John 10:1-16).

There are a lot of believers that attend church but feel harassed and helpless, going to church all the time but not changing or getting anywhere with their relationship with Me. My power can change these people's lives.

This present religious system harasses people and they are helpless, harassed by religious leaders and traditions that do nothing to help a person in this life. They are sheep without a true Shepherd and I am trying to change that.

You need to pray against the religious spirit and complacency in the body of Christ. You need to pray life and encouragement for people and restoration to them, showing them My love and My mercy and compassion. You can do this through Me because I am in you and rest upon you.

Father, help me to see others as You see them praying life, love, and restoration to them as I minister mercy and compassion to them by Your Spirit and power. In Jesus' name Amen.

DAY 6
Read Matthew 9:35-38

If you think about what you are praying, your prayers will not be very effective. You need to be praying by My Spirit flowing through you not praying out of your mind.

You need to trust Me that I am flowing through you and getting to the person what that person needs. You need to be moved by compassion, mercy and love and I will do the rest. I know what is needed and I know what words are needed in prayer, you just need to be the vessel I can pour out of to the person.

Father, I declare Your Spirit flows out of me to pray what is needed in people's hearts and lives. I do not pray from my mind but from my spirit. In Jesus' name Amen.

DAY 7 - SUMMARY
Read Matthew 9:35-38

Whether you are praying for a person one on one or in your personal prayer time, you need to have My love and compassion for that person. You need to seek Me for the specific needs to pray for and allow My Spirit to direct you as you pray.

In personal prayer time, you need to pray in the Spirit, in your prayer language, and My Spirit will pray through you exactly what is needed.

Father, You are my Shepherd and You will lead and guide me as I pray and intercede for those who are hurting and helpless. I love You and praise You Lord. In Jesus' name Amen.

NOTES:

જ⁊જ⁊જ⁊જ⁊જ⁊જ⁊જ⁊જ⁊જ⁊જ⁊જ⁊જ⁊

WEEK 9
❖LOVE ONE ANOTHER❖

જ⁊જ⁊જ⁊જ⁊જ⁊જ⁊જ⁊જ⁊જ⁊જ⁊જ⁊જ⁊

DAY 1
Read John 13:34-35

I know you feel that you can't love others as I love you but I wouldn't command you to do something without giving you the ability to do it. You can love others as I love you because I dwell within you and I will love through you if you allow Me to.

I am love and I love you so much more than you can imagine. As My representatives on the earth, you are to love one another. There are many passages in the My Word about love. As you study them you will learn about My love.

Father, I declare I will love one another as You love me. I will allow Your love to flow through me. In Jesus' name Amen.

DAY 2
Read John 13:34-35

This love for one another is not a matter of emotion as it is of doing things for the benefit of another person, that is, having an unselfish concern for another and a willingness to seek the best for another.

That is agape love, My unconditional love for all. You are to love others unconditionally as I love you. Without Me, this is impossible.

Father, I desire to walk in this agape love for others. Help me to know You more and know Your love that abounds in me. I know it is not by how I feel but knowing this love dwells within me wanting to come out to love others. In Jesus' name Amen.

DAY 3
Read John 13:34-35

You can't be selfish and have love for others. You have to become empty of yourself to love others as I love you. Selfishness is not of Me. It is seeking or concentrating on one's own advantage, pleasure, or wellbeing without regard for others.

Selfishness is the act of being concerned only with oneself. Your focus should be on Me and My Word and not on yourself. If you focus on Me and others, I will take care of you.

Father, forgive me for being selfish a lot of times, not being concerned for those around me. I declare I will not be selfish but will love others as You love me. In Jesus' name Amen.

DAY 4
Read John 13:34-35

Having compassion, being humble and loving others goes hand in hand. It's hard to have compassion with someone if you don't have love for others. You need to love first, and then the compassion will come.

To love and have compassion, you have to be humble before Me so that My love and compassion can flow through you. Compassion means sympathy, usually granted because of unusual or distressing circumstances. I was moved with compassion for the people because they were like sheep without a shepherd.

Father, I declare I will walk in Your love and have compassion on others who are hurting and need to see Your love. In Jesus' name Amen.

DAY 5
Read John 13:34-35

You will be known as my disciple if you love one another because I am love and you need to love as I love. You need to die to self to be able to love as I love because My love is selfless.

You can't love if you're selfish. If you want to be known as My disciple, walking in love and having unselfish concern for others is the only way. Show more interest in others than in yourself.

Father, I declare others will know I am Your disciple by the love and unselfish concern I have for others. In Jesus' name Amen.

DAY 6
Read John 13:34-35

You need to see people as I see them. You are to feel their hurt and have My love and compassion for them. I am giving you a new commandment. This commandment sums up all the commandments of the Old Testament. Love one another as I love you.

If you walk in My love, you will fulfill My commandment and you will be blessed and others will see that love in you and they will know you are My disciple.

I declare I will fulfill the commandment of love by allowing You to flow through me to others and have compassion on them and have unselfish concern for them to help them. I desire to pray and help others as the Spirit leads. In Jesus' name Amen.

DAY 7- SUMMARY
Read John 13:34-35

I have commanded you to love one another as I love you. This will show others that you are My disciple; if you love them you are to have compassion on them. You are to imitate Me in everything.

How can you know Me and My love? By studying and meditating on My life in the Gospels. Learn how I ministered to others and how I walked in agape love. I have poured My love in your hearts to release into other people's lives.

Thank You Father, for Your Word and for Your unconditional love. It's amazing love that dwells within me and wants to flow out of me to others as well as the compassion that You had for hurting people. Flow through me Lord, Your love and compassion as I pray and minister to others. In Jesus' name Amen.

NOTES:

ややややややややややややややややややややや

WEEK 10
❖BE HUMBLE BEFORE GOD❖

ややややややややややややややややややややや

DAY 1
Read James 4:6-10

Being humble describes a person who is devoid of all arrogance and self-exaltation, conceit and haughtiness. A person who is willingly submitted to Me and My will. I oppose the proud. A proud person feels pleasure or satisfaction over something regarded as highly honorable or creditable to oneself; showing a high opinion of one's own dignity, importance, or superiority.

You need to not think that you are better than anyone else. Actually, My Word says not to be selfish; don't try to impress others. Be humble, thinking of others as better than yourself (Philippians 4:3 NLT).

Father, help me to be humble before You and not be self-centered thinking only of myself but to think of others better than myself. In Jesus' name Amen.

DAY 2
Read James 4:6-10

If you are humble, not exalting yourself in any way, I will lift you up. I will raise you up and exalt you. In My Word I warn you that exalting yourself will result in a disgraceful fall, but humbling yourself leads to exaltation in this and the next world.

I will exalt you or raise you up and give you honor, power, character and elevate you to a higher place in Me. Those who are humble receive My grace and are given the secrets of the kingdom, because they come as beggars.

I declare I will not exalt myself but will stay humble before God and allow Him to raise me up and exalt me. Thank You Lord. In Jesus' name Amen.

DAY 3
Read James 4:6-10

I will also give the gift of grace or divine influence upon your heart and favor to those who are humble. I give you the ability to be humble. I will give you the grace if you desire it.

You are to resist the devil and he will flee from you but you must humble yourself first, being submissive to Me. In being humble before Me, I give you the authority to resist the devil and he will flee. I will not resist him for you, you must resist him. Don't say, "Lord, get the devil off of me." I have given you the authority and power to resist him.

Father, thank You for Your grace as I humble myself and submit to You and Your Word. I declare I will resist the Devil and he will flee from me. In Jesus' name Amen.

DAY 4
Read James 4:6-10

I am a jealous God. I want you to be totally devoted to Me and be humble before Me and not become proud. When you think you can do things on your own, that is being proud and I will resist the proud.

I want you to submit to Me and draw near to Me. As you draw near to Me I will draw near to you. Seek Me and you will find Me. I yearn for you to draw near to Me and be humble.

You cannot divide your loyalty between Me and the world. If you do, you are unsettled as a wave of the sea that is blown and tossed by the wind. You are unstable in all your ways and can't expect to receive anything from Me (James 1:8).

Father, I want to draw near to You and be humble before You. I surrender my life to You Lord. I can do nothing without Your Spirit guiding me. I declare I will stay devoted to You not dividing my loyalty between You and the world. In Jesus' name Amen.

DAY 5
Read James 4:6-10

True faith is being humble and humility is the opposite of the proud. Selfishness and self-centered ambition characterizes this present evil age.

Self-centeredness is the highest form of worldliness. Therefore, to be a self-centered person is to be at enmity or hostile and antagonistic with Me. I call for believers to humble themselves before Me.

Father, I don't want to be at enmity with You. I want to be humble before You. I do not want to be self-centered. 2 Chronicles 15:2 says, "The Lord is with you while you are with Him. If you seek Him, He will be found by you; but if you forsake Him, He will forsake you." I declare I will seek You Lord and find You. I will never forsake You. In Jesus' name Amen.

DAY 6
Read James 4:6-10

To be humble, you need to give it all up and hit bottom and let there be tears for what you have done. Let there be sorrow and grief. You need to be doing this more and become totally empty of yourself.

You need to get more serious about Me. You need to get on your knees and cry out to Me, become humble and empty before Me. You need to discern what is in your heart and see through My eyes and see what your motives are and what you need to get rid of.

Father, cleanse me and purify my heart Lord. I want to empty myself and be cleansed of all sins. Show me what is not of You so that I can repent of those things and I can humble myself before You and be lifted up in honor. I declare I will get more serious about You Lord and stop playing games and be humble before You. In Jesus' name Amen.

DAY 7 - SUMMARY
Read James 4:6-10

To come before Me in prayer, you need to be humble before Me, submit your will to Me and I will lift you up.

You need to resist the devil and He will flee. Don't expect Me to resist him for you. You must draw near to Me. Always be hungry for My Presence and I will draw near to you. Be sorrowful for your sins, repent and turn away from them and I will lift you up and exalt you.

Father, thank You for Your grace that You give to the humble and for drawing near to me as I humble myself before You and seek Your face. I love You and praise Your Holy Name. In Jesus' name Amen.

NOTES:

WEEK 11
❖PRAY AT ALL TIMES❖

DAY 1
Read Ephesians 6:10-18; Acts 2:1-4

Prayer "in My Spirit" is any prayer that is directed, energized, and sustained by My Spirit.

Praying in My Spirit: 1. will be according to My will (1 John 5:14-15) 2. will glorify our Father through Me (John 14:13) 3. is based upon My character, ways, and My Word (John 15:7) 4. comes from a clean heart (James 5:16) 5. is prayed in full assurance of faith (James1:6) 6. is asked in My name (John14:14) 7. praying in tongues. Such prayer will always find My answers.

Father, help me to pray more in the Spirit with all prayer and petition with specific requests on every occasion and in every season. In Jesus' name Amen.

DAY 2
Read Ephesians 6:10-18; Acts 2:1-4

You need to stay alert to those around you and discern things going on and intercede in prayer for all people. How can you intercede for all the saints?

The only way you can pray for all My people is by praying in tongues as My Spirit leads. I have given you a spirit language, called praying in tongues or being baptized in My Spirit. It is a gift to you, if you will accept it.

Father, help me to be more alert and discerning of things around me and people who are hurting and needing Your love and compassion and prayer. In Jesus' name Amen.

DAY 3
Read Ephesians 6:10-18; Acts 2:1-4

When you receive Me as your Lord and Savior, you receive My Holy Spirit in your heart. As seen in Acts 2:1-4, the disciples were in one accord in the upper room and My Spirit came upon them and they were all filled with My Holy Spirit and began to speak in other languages (tongues) as My Spirit gave them utterance. This was the beginning of praying in tongues.

It's very important to be able to speak in tongues because it is actually your spirit praying with My Spirit. You may not always know what you are praying but I always know what you are praying and My Spirit will take it to the Father and it will be answered. I will give you the interpretation if you ask. It's especially important because the devil doesn't know what you are praying and that gives you an advantage.

Father, fill me with the Holy Spirit with the evidence of speaking in tongues so that I can pray more effectively and pray perfect prayers because You are praying through me. I declare I will edify myself when needed by praying in the Spirit. Thank You, Lord, for giving me this ability and filling me to overflowing. In Jesus' name Amen.

DAY 4
Read Ephesians 6:10-18; Acts 2:1-4

Praying is part of your spiritual armor. You are to fight in My Spirit for yourselves and for others. You are to be alert; keeping your eyes open so you will be aware of what's going on around you. My Spirit will give you discernment and lead you to pray with all kinds of prayers and requests. My Spirit may lead you to pray in tongues because your words are limited.

Father, I want to learn more of You and Your Word and I declare I will find Scriptures about tongues and different kinds of prayer and study them for my own benefit. In Jesus' name Amen.

DAY 5
Read Ephesians 6:10-18; Acts 2:1-4

To be able to pray in My Spirit on all occasions you need the rest of the spiritual armor because without the full armor of God, you cannot stand against the devil's schemes.

You are to stand firm with the belt of truth buckled around your waist, the breastplate of righteousness in place, feet fitted with the readiness that comes with the gospel of peace. You are to take up the shield of faith. You are to take the helmet of salvation and the sword of My Spirit which is My Word and pray in My Spirit on all occasions. It all goes together for it to work.

Father, thank You for the armor that You provide. I need the full armor to be successful in my prayers and my walk with You. I declare I will put it on daily. In Jesus name Amen.

DAY 6
Read Ephesians 6:10-18; Acts 2:1-4

I provide this armor but you are to put it on. I cannot put it on you. You are to put this armor on in order to stand against the forces of hell. Your warfare is not against physical forces, but against invisible powers who have clearly defined levels of authority in a real, though invisible, sphere of activity. You are to take up the whole armor of God in order to maintain a "battle-stance" against this unseen satanic structure.

All of this armor is not just a passive protection in facing the enemy; it is to be used offensively against these satanic forces. To put on this armor is to prepare for battle. Prayer is the battle itself, with My Word being your chief weapon given against Satan during your struggle.

Father, I declare I will put on the whole armor of God and will stand against the forces of hell. I will use Your Word against the enemy as it is my chief weapon against Satan. In Jesus' name Amen.

ન્ન્ન્ન્ન્ન્ન્ન્ન્ન્ન્ન

DAY 7 – SUMMARY
Read Ephesians 6:10-18; Acts 2:1-4

You are to put on the full armor of God which includes praying in the Spirit on all occasions with all kinds of prayers and requests with Me giving you the words to pray. Praying in My Spirit includes praying in tongues. You must put on this armor. I cannot do it for you.

You are to have a discerning spirit and be alert and praying for My people with love and compassion.

Father, I declare I put on the full armor of God and I am alert and pray with perseverance and intercede in prayer for all God's people. Thank You, Lord, for the leading of Your Spirit and the ability to pray in the Spirit as You lead me in love and compassion. In Jesus' name Amen.

NOTES:

≈≈≈≈≈≈≈≈≈≈≈≈≈≈≈≈≈≈≈≈≈≈≈≈≈

WEEK 12
❖CALL TO HIM❖

≈≈≈≈≈≈≈≈≈≈≈≈≈≈≈≈≈≈≈≈≈≈≈≈≈

DAY 1
Read Jeremiah 33:3; Psalm 4:3; Psalm 6:9; 1 Corinthians 12

Call out to Me as you pray and I will give you the words to say and a discerning Spirit.

I want you to call out to Me when you have a need or when you are praying for others and don't know exactly what to pray for. I will hear and I will answer you. I give you ears to hear My voice.

Father, I call out to You and You will give me the words to pray and a discerning spirit. In Jesus' name Amen.

DAY 2
Read Jeremiah 33:3; Psalm 4:3; Psalm 6:9; 1 Corinthians 12

The positive assurance from Me is that if you will ask Me, I will tell you great and mighty things that you do not know and answer you in ways that will astound you.

I love you and want to show you great and mighty things. John 16:13 says My Holy Spirit will tell you about the future. All you need to do is call out to Me.

Father, thank You for telling me the great and mighty things that I do not know as I call out to You. You will answer me in astounding ways. In Jesus' name Amen.

DAY 3
Read Jeremiah 33:3; Psalm 4:3; Psalm 6:9; 1 Corinthians 12

I listen and answer when you call to Me. I hear your pleas; I will answer your prayer.

I am waiting for you to call out to Me. There are hidden things that I want to show you. I will hear you and answer your pleas.

Father, I declare You listen to me and hear when I call to You. Thank You for hearing and answering me and showing me the hidden things I do not know. In Jesus' name Amen.

DAY 4
Read Jeremiah 33:3; Psalm 4:3; Psalm 6:9; 1 Corinthians 12

I will show you great and mighty things that are fenced in and hidden which you do not distinguish and recognize, have knowledge of or understand. As you cry out to Me, I will answer you.

Come to Me in faith, not doubting because without faith it is impossible to please Me.

Father, I come to You in faith, calling out to You to show me these hidden things that I do not know about. In Jesus' name Amen.

❧❧❧❧❧❧❧❧❧❧❧

DAY 5
Read Jeremiah 33:3; Psalm 4:3; Psalm 6:9; 1 Corinthians 12

There are a lot of things that you do not know or understand. When you call out to Me, I will answer you. How will I answer? I will answer you mostly by My Word. I will give you Scripture to look up and study.

Every hidden thing is in My Word. You just need to ask Me and I will show You. Study and present yourself to Me approved and correctly analyze and accurately divide the Word of truth (2 Timothy 2:15)

Father, I declare the hidden things You want to tell me are in Your Word and You will show me where to find those things. In Jesus' name Amen.

❧❧❧❧❧❧❧❧❧❧❧

DAY 6
Read Jeremiah 33:3; Psalm 4:3; Psalm 6:9; 1 Corinthians 12

I will hear you and answer when you call to Me about someone you are praying about. I desire to give you insight and revelation. I desire every believer to operate in the gifts of the Spirit which are listed in 1 Corinthians 12.

A spiritual gift is given to each of you so you can help each other. Desire these gifts and ask Me for them and I will give them to you. I alone decide which gift each person should have.

Father, thank You for hearing me and answering me when I call. I ask for Your spiritual gifts to manifest in my life as You see fit. In Jesus' name Amen.

DAY 7 - SUMMARY
Read Jeremiah 33:3; Psalm 4:3; Psalm 6:9; 1 Corinthians 12

I desire for you to call out to Me in faith and I will answer and show you great and mighty things. There are many things I want to show you that are hidden and you have no knowledge or understanding of.

I want to give you insight and revelation knowledge of My Word. Call out to Me, come to Me in faith. Study the gifts of the Spirit and desire them and I will show you and help manifest them in your life.

Father, I declare I call to You and You will answer me with things I do not know or understand and You will give me the gifts of the Spirit as I seek them and study them. Thank You, Lord, for giving me the best things in my life. In Jesus' name Amen.

NOTES:

⫷⫷⫷⫷⫷⫷⫷⫷⫷⫷⫷⫷⫷⫷⫷⫷⫷⫷⫷⫷⫷⫷⫷⫷⫷⫷

WEEK 13
❖PRAYER OFFERED IN FAITH❖

⫷⫷⫷⫷⫷⫷⫷⫷⫷⫷⫷⫷⫷⫷⫷⫷⫷⫷⫷⫷⫷⫷⫷⫷⫷⫷

DAY 1
Read James 5:13-18; Hebrews 11:1, 6; Mark 11:22-23

Faith is the confidence of the things you hope for will actually happen; it gives you assurance of things you cannot see.

You may not see your answer in the natural realm immediately but your faith knows that I answered in the spirit realm and it will manifest in the natural as long as you stay in faith.

Without faith you cannot please Me. You have to believe I exist and that I am a rewarder of those who diligently seek Me.

Father, I declare I come to You in faith when I pray. I will not doubt but believe in You and You will reward me as I diligently seek You. In Jesus' name Amen.

DAY 2
Read James 5:13-18; Hebrews 11:1, 6; Mark 11:22-23

Now faith is… Now is in the present. Hope is in the future. Saying you hope so is future tense. You have to have faith for what you are hoping for. Have faith in Me constantly.

You need to speak to the mountain (the problem) in faith, not doubting and it will be thrown into the sea. Don't talk about the problem, talk to it.

Father, I declare I talk to my problems rather than about them. In Jesus' name Amen.

ৡৡৡৡৡৡৡৡৡৡৡৡ

DAY 3
Read James 5:13-18; Hebrews 11:1, 6; Mark 11:22-23

Your prayer of faith will save the person, who is sick, and I will restore him and his sins will be forgiven. It is My will that you be healthy so that you can minister as I lead you.

Confess your sins to one another and pray for one another. I want none to perish and I am a forgiving God.

Father, I declare I pray in faith for the sick and they will be healed and restored. In Jesus' name Amen.

ৡৡৡৡৡৡৡৡৡৡৡৡ

DAY 4
Read James 5:13-18; Hebrews 11:1, 6; Mark 11:22-23

Fervent prayer is having or showing great warmth or intensity of spirit, feeling, enthusiasm, etc., being ardent, hot, burning, and glowing. The earnest prayer is serious in intention, purpose, or effort; sincerely zealous.

You are righteous in My sight which is being in right standing with Me. You are righteous if you have accepted Me as your Lord and Savior and surrendered your life to Me

Effective prayer is characterized by earnestness, fervency and energy. Put energy behind your prayers.

Father, I declare I am fervent in my prayers. I put energy into my prayers and they are effective. In Jesus' name Amen.

DAY 5
Read James 5:13-18; Hebrews 11:1, 6; Mark 11:22-23

James pictures a level of prayer that is beyond any believers' normal capacity; it is divinely energized by the direct involvement of My Spirit. Your praying energized by the power of My Spirit causes things to happen. Your prayers work! It is dynamic in its working.

It says the prayer of a righteous man makes tremendous power available. If you are My child, you are righteous in My eyes so don't say your prayers are not powerful or effective.

Father, I declare that my praying is energized by the power of the Holy Spirit which causes things to happen. In Jesus' name Amen.

DAY 6
Read James 5:13-18; Hebrews 11:1, 6; Mark 11:22-23

Elijah is like you and he prayed earnestly for it not to rain and no rain fell on the earth for 3 ½ years (I Kings 17:1). Then he prayed again for rain and it rained; he had faith in Me for it to happen. You are able to pray and be effective just as Elijah.

Father, as Elijah, I will earnestly and fervently pray and believe what I'm praying for will happen. In Jesus' name Amen.

DAY 7 - SUMMARY
Read James 5:13-18; Hebrews 11:1, 6; Mark 11:22-23

Have faith in Me and not doubt when praying and the sick person will be made well and I will raise him up. If he has sinned, I will forgive him.

Your prayers are effective through My Spirit, energizing them. My Spirit will make things happen if you are in faith and do not doubt. Allow My Spirit to flow through you energizing your prayers.

I declare I have faith and will not doubt. The prayer of faith will make the sick person well. Thank You for energizing my prayers to be effective. In Jesus' name Amen.

NOTES:

≈≈≈≈≈≈≈≈≈≈≈≈≈≈≈≈≈≈≈≈≈≈

WEEK 14
❖EXAMINE YOURSELF❖

≈≈≈≈≈≈≈≈≈≈≈≈≈≈≈≈≈≈≈≈≈≈

DAY 1
Read 2 Corinthians 13:5-6; Hebrews 11:1, 6

It says to examine, test and evaluate your own selves to see whether you are holding to your faith and showing the proper fruits of it. How do you examine yourself? Check your heart with My Word to make sure it lines up with what My Word is saying.

If you are at all in controversy to what My Word is saying about something then you are not in faith. Always evaluate your heart according to My Word not by other people and their faith or actions.

Father, I declare I will examine, test and evaluate myself whether I am solid in my faith. In Jesus' name Amen

DAY 2
Read 2 Corinthians 13:5-6; Hebrews 11:1, 6

What is faith? It shows the reality of what you hope for; it is the evidence of things you cannot see. Faith is now; hope is future tense. It is impossible to please Me without faith.

Anyone who wants to come to Me must believe that I exist and that I reward those who sincerely seek Me. Have faith when you pray. I will not hear your prayers if you are not in faith. Test yourself to make sure you are in faith.

Father, I will examine myself to make sure I am solid in my faith. I want to please You by having faith and I believe You exist and reward me because I seek You. In Jesus' name Amen.

DAY 3
Read 2 Corinthians 13:5-6; Hebrews 11:1, 6

Do not drift along taking everything for granted. Do you take things for granted? Do you just assume everything is ok with your relationship with Me because you feel you are strong in your faith? If you get your focus off Me onto worldly things, worldly news and allow fear to enter into your heart that will affect your faith and your relationship with Me.

You have to give yourself regular checkups. Get into My Word and stay in faith and do not take things for granted.

Father, I don't want to take anything for granted, especially You Lord. I want to stay focused on You and Your Word and stay in faith. In Jesus' name Amen.

DAY 4
Read 2 Corinthians 13:5-6; Hebrews 11:1, 6

What is firsthand evidence that I am in you? If you are My child, then I am in you. You will not always feel My presence but you must believe that I dwell within you. You have to know that you are the temple of My Spirit and that My Spirit lives in you (1 Corinthians 3:16).

If you do not know this, do something about it by seeking Me and My Word. Get that revelation that you are My temple and that you are holy because I live in you. You have to have the faith because you don't always feel My presence but I live in you and will never leave you.

Father, I desire a revelation that You live in me that I am Your temple and You make me holy because You live in me. In Jesus' name Amen.

ৡৡৡৡৡৡৡৡৡৡৡ

DAY 5
Read 2 Corinthians 13:5-6; Hebrews 11:1, 6

You need to give yourself regular checkups to make sure you are solid in the faith. Do you pray in faith? How do you check up on yourself? You check up on yourself by meditating on My Word. Do you have doubts when you read My Word? You must have faith in Me constantly (Mark 11:22) and not doubt.

When you pray for something, don't immediately speak negative things or the opposite of what you prayed for. Stay in faith. Get into My Word and speak My Word, not your doubts.

If you need healing, find Scriptures on healing and confess them rather than speaking the physical problem. I am greater than any physical problem. I am greater than cancer, I am greater than arthritis. I am the great physician and I want every one of My children to be in health.

Father, I want to pray in faith and stay in faith. I declare I will get in Your Word and stay in Your Word until my faith is where it should be. In Jesus' name Amen.

ৡৡৡৡৡৡৡৡৡৡৡ

DAY 6
Read 2 Corinthians 13:5-6; Hebrews 11:1, 6

You need to examine yourself to see if your loyalty, strength, opinions, disposition, condition, faith, patience and character is as mine. Don't let things that are not of Me get in the way of your relationship with Me. Your relationship with Me should be the most important thing in your life.

Do not quench My Spirit that lives in you by having wrong motives. You are holy because I am holy and I live in you. I want to be first in your life and I want you to hunger for My Word and put it first in your life so that your faith in Me will be solid.

Father, I declare I examine myself to see if my loyalty, strength, opinions, disposition, condition, faith, patience and character is as Yours. I declare I am in the faith and if not, I will get into Your Word until I am in faith. In Jesus' name Amen.

DAY 7 - SUMMARY
Read 2 Corinthians 13:5-6; Hebrews 11:1, 6

In summary, you are to examine yourself to make sure you are solid in the faith and that you have the fruit of faith in your life. Don't take things or Me for granted.

Give yourself regular checkups to stay in faith and walk as I walked. You need the revelation that I live in you and that you are the temple of My Holy Spirit. I will always be with you whether you feel My presence or not. Have faith in Me constantly.

Father, I declare I will examine myself daily to make sure I am solid in my faith. If I am not, I will get into Your Word until my faith is solid in every circumstance. In Jesus' name Amen.

NOTES:

WEEK 15
❖AUTHORITY IN JESUS' NAME❖

DAY 1
Read Luke 10:1-20

I sent out 70 of My disciples two by two to the surrounding towns to tell about Me, heal the sick and tell them My kingdom is near them. Then they returned with joy saying "even the demons are subject to us in Your name".

I sent them out two by two in My name. It's important to go out two by two rather than by yourself. They came back excited because in My name the demons were subject to them. They were amazed at what had happened. I give you that same authority in My name against the demons and against sickness and disease.

Father, I declare the demons are subject to me in Jesus' name. Thank You for the power and authority in Your name. In Jesus' name Amen.

DAY 2
Read Luke 10:1-20

I saw Satan fall like lightning from heaven when the disciples defeated Satan in My name. Satan is defeated in My name. The devil only has power that you allow him to have.

Since a lot of you are not aware that you have power and authority over the devil in My name, you are defeated. You are waiting on Me to do something but I am waiting on you because I have already defeated the devil by My shed blood on the cross and I rose from the grave to give you the victory.

Father, I declare the devil is defeated in my life because of Your name and Your blood shed on the cross. You defeated him and I have the victory. In Jesus' name Amen.

DAY 3
Read Luke 10:1-20

I have given you authority and power to trample upon serpents and scorpions, and (physical and mental strength and ability) over all the power that the enemy possesses; and nothing shall in any way harm you.

Because I give you this power and authority, you have a responsibility to use this authority I have given you. I cannot get the devil out of your life. You have My power and authority and the responsibility to command the devil out of your life. If you pray without the authority, you will not have effective prayer and the devil will defeat you.

Father, thank You for the power and authority Jesus gives us in His name. I declare I will use the name of Jesus to defeat the devil and will see him fall from heaven and have the victory. In Jesus' name Amen.

DAY 4
Read Luke 10:1-20

I said that nothing shall in any way harm you. That should be a comfort to you with everything that is going on today. You need to believe My Word and confess that nothing shall in any way harm you.

My Spirit dwells within you. I am always there and I will protect you and keep you from harm but you must stand firm in your faith and use the power and authority I have given you to defeat the devil and the evil around you.

Father, I declare that nothing shall in any way harm me. That includes terrorists as well as sickness and disease. In Your name, I have victory over these things and over all the power that the enemy possesses. In Jesus' name Amen.

DAY 5
Read Luke 10:1-20

You are not to rejoice in the fact that the demons are subject to the power I give you but to rejoice that your name is in the Book of life. Just knowing your name is in the Book of life and that you are enrolled in heaven should give you reason to rejoice.

Don't get prideful or think you are something great when you use My authority and power against demons and they are subject to you. You are My representative on the earth and a vessel I work through. I give you the power and authority in My name to give you the victory.

Father, I rejoice that my name is in the Book of life. I thank You that I have eternal life. I am also thankful for the power and authority in Jesus' name that is given to me to defeat the devil. I declare I will not get prideful thinking I am something great because the demons are subject to me. In Jesus' name Amen.

DAY 6
Read Luke 10:1-20

I have given you power and authority, physical and mental strength and ability over all the power that the enemy possesses. Get this revelation and realize who you are and what you have in My name. The devil is under your feet and you can have the victory over him in every area of your life.

Get into My Word and find out what you have in My name. You have reason to rejoice because you are given everything you need for life and godliness.

Father, I declare I have physical and mental strength and ability over all the power the enemy possesses. I will get into the Word and find out who I am and what I have in Christ. In Jesus' name Amen.

∽∽∽∽∽∽∽∽∽∽∽

DAY 7 – SUMMARY
Read Luke 10:1-20

When I send you out, it is always two by two. I give you the power and authority over all the power the enemy possesses only in My name. You cannot do it without Me nor without using My name.

My name is powerful and the demons know My name and tremble because of My name. Do not get prideful thinking you are something great because the demons are subject to you because it is only through My name you have the victory.

Rejoice that your name is in the Book of life and you are enrolled in heaven.

Thank You, Father, for the power and authority in Jesus' name and that the demons are subject to me in that name. Thank You that my name is in the Book of life and heaven is my eternal home. In Jesus' name Amen.

NOTES:

WEEK 16
❖HAVE FAITH IN GOD❖

DAY 1
Read Mark 11:15-25; Hebrews 11:6

Have faith in Me constantly. This means to have My kind of faith which is conviction, confidence, trust, belief, reliance, trustworthiness, and persuasion.

It is impossible to please Me without faith. Anyone who wants to come to Me must believe that I exist and that I reward those who sincerely seek Me. You had faith when you asked Me into your life; it's the same faith.

Father, I want to please You. Thank You for giving me Your faith and I can be victorious in all things because You reward those who have faith and diligently seek You. In Jesus' name Amen

DAY 2
Read Mark 11:15-25; Hebrews 11:6

You are to speak to your mountain or your problem and tell it to be removed and cast into the sea. I give you the power and authority to do this. I cannot cast your mountain into the sea. If you do not doubt in your heart but believe what you say, you will have whatever you say.

You must believe and not doubt what you say. This can work in the negative also. If you say something like, "I'm going to catch the flu. I do every year around this time". If you say it enough and believe it, guess what? You'll get the flu. What you say matters. Death and life are in the power of the tongue, and they who indulge in it shall eat the fruit of it [for death or life] (Proverbs 18:21). Choose life!

Father, thank You, that I have a choice to speak life or death into my life and into other people's lives. I declare I choose life today. In Jesus' name Amen.

ख़ख़ख़ख़ख़ख़ख़ख़ख़ख़ख़

DAY 3
Read Mark 11:15-25; Hebrews 11:6

Your mountain can be any obstacle that is blocking your relationship with Me. You can cast the mountain into the sea by speaking to it in My name. I give you authority to speak against the mountain, against the devil (Matthew 10:8; James 4:7), against sickness and disease, against lack, against anything that is not of Me.

Father, thank You for the authority You give me in Jesus' name to cast the mountain into the sea. I declare I will speak positive things, not negative things. In Jesus' name Amen.

ख़ख़ख़ख़ख़ख़ख़ख़ख़ख़ख़

DAY 4
Read Mark 11:15-25; Hebrews 11:6

Whatever you ask and believe for, it will be granted to you. Ask for things that are My will and things that glorify Me.

How do you know My will? Read My Word. You'll find everything you need in it. Ask in faith without wavering because if you are in doubt you are double minded and you will not receive from Me the things you asked for (James 1:6).

Father, I will ask only what is Your will and I believe that I receive what I have asked for without doubting. In Jesus' name Amen.

DAY 5
Read Mark 11:15-25; Hebrews 11:6

When you are praying you need to forgive anyone you have a grudge against, otherwise I will not forgive you or hear your prayers. You must have a heart of forgiveness.

I have forgiven you and you must do likewise. I will not hear your prayers if you are in un-forgiveness.

Help me Lord to forgive others as You have forgiven me. I declare I will walk in forgiveness continually. In Jesus' name Amen.

DAY 6
Read Mark 11:15-25; Hebrews 11:6

It's hard for some people to forgive those who hurt them. Holding a grudge is only hurting you. It doesn't affect the other person. Holding a grudge can cause bitterness. When you become bitter, it affects your health and attitude. It can cause your heart to harden and pushes Me away. Ask Me to help you to forgive. Be willing to forgive and I will soften your heart.

You must repent of un-forgiveness because it is a sin. Release the offender from your judgment. You are not to judge others (Matthew 7:1-2). You can trust Me to judge righteously as you forgive and walk in love. Bless those you are forgiving until you're feelings toward them have changed (Luke 6:27-28). Bless them by praying for them and speaking blessing over them.

Father, I declare I will walk in love and forgiveness and hold no grudges against anyone. In Jesus' name Amen.

❧❧❧❧❧❧❧❧❧❧❧

DAY 7 - SUMMARY
Read Mark 11:15-25; Hebrews 11:6

How do these verses relate to prayer? You must have faith when you pray. You can speak to the mountain and not doubt and you will have what you say. I have given you authority in My name to cast the mountain into the sea. Watch what you say. Speak positive things, speak what you desire, not what you have.

Stop speaking the problem and speak to the problem. Have faith and you'll have what you say. Forgiveness is important as you pray because if you are in un-forgiveness or are bitter, it will block Me from hearing you. If you don't seem to have results in your praying, check your heart and make sure you have forgiven everyone. Forgive and you will receive.

Thank You, Father that I have the God kind of faith and I can speak to my mountains. As I do, they will be cast into the sea. As I forgive those who have hurt me, You will forgive me and hear me as I speak. Thank You Lord, I love and praise You. In Jesus' name Amen.

NOTES:

WEEK 17
❖DECLARE THE DECREE❖

DAY 1
Read Psalm 2:6-9; Job 22:28

Declare or state firmly and decree or command My Word. Of course, you need to study My Word and know it to declare it. In all the accounts of ministering to people, I spoke a Word and it was done. I didn't stand and pray many words over the person.

I spent many hours alone praying to our Father, which you need to do also. By spending hours with our Father, I knew Him and did only what He said to do.

Father, I declare I will spend time in Your Word, meditating and studying it so I know what You are saying to me and I am able to do it. In Jesus' name Amen.

DAY 2
Read Psalm 2:6-9; Job 22:28

There are many places in Scripture showing how I ministered to people. In the Luke 13:12 account I healed the woman who was bent over. I spoke the word and it was done. How would you minister to someone who was bent over like this woman? Most of you would stand there and pray asking Me to heal her, to straighten her spine, rebuke the devil, etc. All I did was say, "You are loosed from your infirmity."

You are to do things the same way I did and you will have the same results. You can't operate in fear when you are praying. You need to have the faith and say to the sick, "you are loosed from your infirmity" and place your hands on them and expect them to be healed. You need to know My Word, especially with healing.

I sent My Word to heal you so you don't need to be praying and asking Me to heal. I have already done it. Declare what I have said in My Word. Know My Word and stand in faith.

Father, I declare I know the Word of God and when I pray, I speak the Word and declare it done. In Jesus' name Amen.

DAY 3
Read Psalm 2:6-9; Job 22:28

Another incident where I spoke a word and it was done is in Matthew 9:6-7. I, at first, told the paralytic that his sins were forgiven him but the Pharisees were thinking evil thoughts and I said, "Which is easier to say, your sins are forgiven or get up and walk?" So I said to show I had authority to forgive sins, "to rise up and walk" and he arose and departed.

I am saying that your sins being forgiven and being healed is the same thing. I forgive all your iniquities and heal all your diseases (Psalm 103:3). It is part of the atonement on the cross (Isaiah 53:5). Regarding the paralytic, I spoke the word and it was done. I didn't pray a bunch of words. My Spirit dwells within you and you have the same authority I had and are to do the same things I did and even greater things (John 14:12).

Thank You, Father, that You forgave me my iniquities and healed me by Your death on the cross, You have given me so very much. I declare I will study Your Word so that I know what I have in You. Forgive me for not walking as Jesus walked and doing as Jesus did. In Jesus' name Amen.

DAY 4
Read Psalm 2:6-9; Job 22:28

Peter and John ministered to a crippled man at the gate beautiful. Peter said, "In the name of Jesus Christ of Nazareth, rise up and walk" and Peter took his hand and lifted him up. He stood and started leaping, walking and praising Me (Acts 3:1-8). The disciples did the same thing I did when ministering to others. The disciples used the authority in My name. I didn't have to use My name when I ministered, I was the authority. My point is, the disciples didn't pray for the person, they spoke to the fellow what to do and it was done. He was healed.

Father, help me to trust You more when ministering to people so I can receive results as You received and the disciples received. I declare I will minister in faith and confidence and will see results. In Jesus' name Amen.

∫∫∫∫∫∫∫∫∫∫∫

DAY 5
Read Psalm 2:6-9; Job 22:28

There was a fellow in Luke 5:13 who had leprosy and he said to Me, "If you are willing you are able to cure me and make me clean." I said, "I am willing, be cleansed!" and immediately the leprosy left him.

You are like this fellow; you don't know that I am willing to heal. It is My will to heal. I spoke it and it was done. I didn't pray, "Father, touch this fellow and cleanse him". Remember, you have been given the same power and authority I had. I gave it to the disciples and I gave it to you also to use to operate in and to see results.

Father, my faith is lacking in this area of ministering. I declare I will meditate on the Word of God to increase my faith by Your Word and see results. Thank You, Lord. In Jesus' name Amen.

∫∫∫∫∫∫∫∫∫∫∫

DAY 6
Read Psalm 2:6-9; Job 22:28

Peter's mother-in-law was suffering with a burning fever and they pleaded with Me to heal her. I rebuked the fever, and it left her and she immediately got up and started waiting on us (Luke 4:38-39).

You should be able to rebuke fevers and they leave. You have a child that has a fever, rebuke the fever in My name and it will leave. I didn't pray a long prayer asking our Father to touch her and take the fever away. I spoke to the fever and it left. You can speak to any sickness in your body and it will have to leave, in My name.

Why don't you see the results I and the disciples had? It is unbelief on your part. You fear it won't happen, which it won't if you are praying in fear. You need to know the authority you have in My name to receive results.

I have provided what you need to minister effectively and get results. Don't pray, speak to it.

Thank You, Father, for giving me the authority against sickness and disease in Jesus' name. I declare I will use the authority I have in Jesus against any and all sickness and disease. I will speak to it in Jesus' name and it must leave. In Jesus' name Amen.

DAY 7 - SUMMARY
Read Psalm 2:6-9; Job 22:28

I and the disciples ministered to people by decreeing and declaring and it was done. We didn't pray any prayers, we spoke and it was.

I have given you the power and authority in My name to minister to others effectively with results. You can find many Scriptures showing how I ministered and how the disciples ministered to others with results. Find these and study them until you have them down in your spirit and minister as I and the disciples ministered with results.

Thank You, Father, that You have given me examples that I can follow to minister to others and get results. In Jesus' name Amen.

NOTES:

❧❧❧❧❧❧❧❧❧❧❧❧❧❧❧❧❧❧❧❧❧❧❧❧

WEEK 18
❖DEMAND IN JESUS' NAME❖

❧❧❧❧❧❧❧❧❧❧❧❧❧❧❧❧❧❧❧❧❧❧❧❧

DAY 1
Read John 14:12-14

I know you are probably asking how can you possibly do more than Me? It is only by My Holy Spirit working in and through you as you yield yourself to Me that you are able to do greater things.

The main emphasis of this verse is that you will be able to do all that I did (I John 4:17) I dwell within you and have given you the authority and power I had and expect you to use it and get the same results that I had when I ministered to people.

Thank You, Father, for giving me that power and authority in Jesus' name to overcome the evil in this world and be victorious. I declare I can do the things Jesus did and even greater things because the Holy Spirit lives in me. In Jesus' name Amen.

DAY 2
Read John 14:12-14

Verse 13 says I will do whatever you ask in My name. This word "ask" means demand. You can't demand anything of Me but in My name it gives you the authority to demand demons to flee, sickness to be gone, the curse to be off of your life. Because of Me you are redeemed from the curse but the devil will try to put things in your mind that are not of Me.

I give you the authority in My name to rebuke these things the devil tries to distract you with. You are not to sit back and expect Me to take care of things that I have given you the authority to handle. If you are sick, I have provided healing and in My name you are to take it and command sickness and disease to go and it will go.

Father, thank You for giving to me authority in Jesus' name to use for Your glory and have victory in my life. In Jesus' name Amen.

DAY 3
Read John **14:12-14**

My name, Jesus, is above every name. Every knee will bow to My name as well as every sickness, disease, lack, etc. All authority (all power of rule) in heaven and on earth has been given to Me (Matthew 28:18) and I delegate My authority to the church, to you, and I promised you that "These signs shall follow you that believe: In My name…" (Mark 16:17).

In My name! I authorized you. I gave you My name as the authority. The power is in My name. The authority is in My name. You're authorized to use My name. Go…

Thank You, Father, for giving me the authority and power in Jesus' name in the earth. I declare I will use the authority in His name and will have the victory. In Jesus' name Amen.

DAY 4
Read John **14:12-14**

I AM! I AM all that you need. By using My name you are representing all that I AM. My name represents I AM and glorifies the Father. Our Father identifies Himself as I AM WHO I AM. Revealing His divine name declares His character and attributes, reinforcing that the issue is not who you are, but who is with you and in you.

Do a study on all the names of our Father and get a better understanding of our Father God's character. My name represents the Father as I AM. All that our Father God is I AM and I have given you My name to represent our Father in the earth as I AM.

Thank You, Father, for giving me power and authority in Jesus' name, the I AM representing and glorifying You. In Jesus' name Amen.

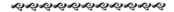

DAY 5
Read John **14:12-14**

When you use My name and take the authority I have given you in My name, it glorifies (honors and praises) our Father because you are obeying Him.

You will receive from Me what you have asked (demanded), in My name. I will do whatever you ask (demand) in My name.

Father, I want to glorify You by using Jesus' name. Thank You for giving Jesus and the authority in His name against the evil one. I declare I have authority in Jesus' name to use against the devil and the evil he tries to put on me. In Jesus' name Amen.

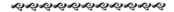

DAY 6
Read John **14:12-14**

I said that I would grant whatever you ask in My name. Whatever you ask for? What you ask for must be what will glorify and extol our Father. You are not to ask for selfish things and things you know My Word speaks against.

Ask what is in My Word. My Word is My will. Healing is My will so you can ask for it and command sickness to be gone in My name. Sickness does not glorify our Father but healing and health does.

Father, I declare that what I ask for will glorify and extol You and Jesus will grant it to me. In Jesus' name Amen.

ৼৼৼৼৼৼৼৼৼৼ

DAY 7 - SUMMARY
Read John 14:12-14

According to these verses you can do all of what I did and even more. There is another verse that states, "As I am so are you in the earth" (1 John 4:17). God, our Father, has given you My name, Jesus, and the authority and power in that name.

Whatever you ask (demand) in My name, I will give it to you. You are not demanding us to do anything; you are demanding the devil and all evil to leave, in My name. You glorify our Father God when you do this. You are representing Me when you use my name.

I AM! In My name is everything you need. I AM whatever you need. All authority is in My name, Jesus. All power is in My name, Jesus. I have given My name so you can have victory on the earth and in your life.

Jesus, I love Your name, Your Holy and precious name. There is something about that name. There's power in that name, there's authority in that name. Every knee has to bow to Your name (Philemon 2:10). Thank You, Father for Jesus and His Holy name. Thank You for the love, power and authority in that name. In Jesus' name Amen.

NOTES:

WEEK 19
❖ASK IN JESUS' NAME❖

DAY 1
Read John 16:20-24

The word "ask" in last week's passage meant demand in My name. This passage in John 16, "ask" means request or petition. It states you will no longer ask Me anything but ask our Father through My name.

I, Jesus, am the way to the Father. While I was on the earth, My disciples did not use My name in prayer. It was after I arose from the dead, the Church, you, is to pray in My name to our Father.

Father, thank You for Jesus making the way to You, through Jesus' name. I love You Father. In Jesus' name Amen.

DAY 2
Read John 16:20-24

In My name, our Father will grant you whatever you ask. You're representing Me on the earth and I am representing you to our Father. I AM anything and everything you need. I gave you the legal right to use My name and it gives our Father great joy to recognize that name.

It is beyond your understanding of the possibilities given in My name. When I gave you the legal right to use My name, our Father knew all that My name would imply when spoken in prayer by oppressed souls, and it is His joy to recognize that name.

So the possibilities enfolded in My name are beyond your understanding, and when I say to the Church, to you, "Whatsoever you shall ask of our Father in My name," I am giving you a signed check on the resources of heaven and asking you to fill it in. Study My Word to see all that My name gives you.

Thank You, Father, for the name of Jesus and the promises within that name. I declare I will study the Scriptures regarding the name of Jesus and learn all that I have in His name. In Jesus' name Amen.

DAY 3
Read John 16:20-24

Asking our Father in My name will give you joy. I have come to give you life and joy (John 10:10). There is so much you can receive in My name. I would like to give a few Scriptures regarding My name and show what you have in My name.

When you use My name, you are saying "Immanuel, God with us" (Matthew 1:23). You can say "in the name of Jesus, God with us, be healed and made whole". You know I am with you but to know that is what My name means should help you to never forget I am with you.

Thank You, Father, for the joy of the Lord in Jesus' name and thank You that You are always with me. Help me to remember that Jesus' name means, God is with me. In Jesus' name Amen.

DAY 4
Read John 16:20-24

You can drive out demons, speak in new languages, pick up serpents and if you drink anything deadly, it will not hurt you; and if you will lay your hands on the sick, they will get well (Mark 16:17-18). You can do all these things in My name.

This doesn't mean pick serpents up to prove your faith but as Paul in Acts when he was bit by a serpent when building a fire, it did not hurt him. The same with drinking anything deadly, it will not hurt you. It's always good to bless your food in My name and nothing shall hurt you. You can lay hands on the sick and they shall recover. There's power and authority in My name.

Thank You, Father, for these signs to follow me, accompany me as I believe in Jesus' name. Thank You for the power and authority You give me. In Jesus' name Amen.

DAY 5
Read John 16:20-24

You can heal others in My name as Peter did. Peter used my name and immediately the cripple rose up and walked. He was healed just by using My name. He didn't pray for the cripple, he spoke in My name and he rose up and walked (Acts 3:6).

It's no wonder you don't have healing and miracles in your Churches. You pray in My name for the people but you don't take the authority I have given you against sickness and disease.

You are in fear that the person won't be healed and you will look bad. You are intimidated by what man thinks. Just trust Me and My Word and imitate Me and the disciples and you will have results.

Father, I declare that I will be bold with the authority You have given me in Jesus' name. Help me to not fear but to trust You and Your Word. In Jesus' name Amen.

DAY 6
Read John 16:20-24

You have salvation in My name and it is only through My name that you are saved (Romans 10:13). I am the only way, truth and life. Every knee will have to bow to My name and every tongue has to confess that I, Jesus Christ, am Lord (Philippians 2:9-11). If you have not made Me your Lord and Savior, I am here for you. Accept Me now and I will give you life abundantly. You will someday bow to Me and confess Me as Lord, willingly and you will go to heaven or unwillingly, you will be cast into the lake of fire.

Every sickness and disease has to bow to My name. Cancer, you're a name and you have to bow to My name because My name is above every name. Arthritis, bursitis, lack, you name it and it has to bow to My name. Whatever you may be suffering from, name it and tell it to bow to My name and be gone because I am above every name. This all gives glory to God our Father.

Father, at the name of Jesus I bow before You and confess that Jesus Christ is Lord. I give You all glory and honor. In Jesus' name Amen.

DAY 7 - SUMMARY
Read John 16:20-24

You are to ask our Father through My name for all you need. I am your mediator and My name is the way. My name means Emmanuel, God with us. That is so important to remember that I am always with you.

There are signs that accompany you in My name. Peter spoke healing in My name. My name is above every name. There are many other verses about My name (James 5:15; I John 3:23; I John 5:13; Revelation 19:12-13, 16; Revelation 22:3-4). Check them out on your own and see the importance of My name and the power and authority you have in My name.

Thank You, Father, for giving me Jesus and His loving and precious name and for the power and authority given to me in Jesus' name. Thank You and praise You Lord. In Jesus' name Amen.

NOTES:

WEEK 20
❖PULLING DOWN STRONGHOLDS❖

DAY 1
Read 2 Corinthians 10:3-6

You walk in the flesh but do not war according to the flesh. You are mortals living in the realities of this world but you do not fight with human weapons.

You are not to fight and argue with your brothers and sisters because the devil is behind every evil intention and strife among others. So your warfare is not against flesh and blood but against evil demonic forces.

Father, I declare I walk in the flesh but do not war according to the flesh for my weapons are not of the flesh but mighty in God. In Jesus' name Amen.

DAY 2
Read 2 Corinthians 10:3-6

Strongholds are first established in your mind; that is why you are to take every thought captive. Behind a stronghold is also a lie, behind a lie is a fear and behind every fear is an idol. An idol is established whenever you fail to trust in My provisions.

How do you take every thought captive? First, you need to know My Word so you know what is not My thoughts (Hebrews 4:12-13). Knowing what My Word says, you can speak against a thought that is contrary to My Word.

Father, I declare I meditate on Your Word and can know what words are contrary to Your Word and take captive of it so it doesn't become strongholds in my mind. In Jesus' name Amen.

DAY 3
Read 2 Corinthians 10:3-6

Another weapon that can be used to pull down strongholds is My blood shed on the cross. You can overcome the devil by My blood and by the word of your testimony (Revelation 12:11). My shed blood on the cross gives you the victory.

Father, Thank You for Jesus' blood shed on the cross for my victory. I declare I overcome by the blood of the Lamb and the word of my testimony. In Jesus' name Amen.

DAY 4
Read 2 Corinthians 10:3-6

Another weapon to pull down strongholds is with My name, Jesus. Signs will follow you who believe: In My name you will cast out demons; you will speak with new tongues; you will take up serpents; and if you drink anything deadly, it will by no means hurt you; you will lay hands on the sick, and they will recover (Mark 16:17-18).

Know who you are in Me and what you have in Me. You will find this all in My Word.

Father, I thank You for the name of Jesus that gives me the power and authority to take captive those thoughts and strongholds against me. In Jesus' name Amen.

DAY 5
Read 2 Corinthians 10:3-6

You are to cast down arguments and every high thing that exalts itself against the knowledge of Me. Arguments would be warfare in your mind, arrogant, rebellious ideas and attitudes. You are to cast these down.

What do I mean by casting them down? If it is contrary to My Word, it is to be cast down, just as I did in the desert. I said "it is written…" (Luke 4:3-12). You must say the same but you need to know My Word to say it.

Father, I declare I know Your Word and when a contrary thought comes I will cast it down by saying, "it is written…" In Jesus' name Amen.

DAY 6
Read 2 Corinthians 10:3-6

Every high thing that you are to cast down would be prideful things. There are a lot of high things that exalt itself against Me in this world today. Some things sound good but the wisdom of the world is not My wisdom so be discerning and led by My Spirit and seek Me to know what My thoughts are.

You must bring every thought into captivity to My obedience. It comes down to knowing My Word.

.

Father, I will take captive every high thing that exalts itself above You and bring every thought into captivity to the obedience of You. In Jesus' name Amen.

DAY 7 - SUMMARY
Read 2 Corinthians 10:3-6

You walk in the flesh but your warfare is not of the flesh. Your mind is the battlefield so you need to cast down arguments, rebellious ideas and attitudes and every high and prideful thing that exalts itself against Me. You are to take every thought into captivity to My obedience.

So you need to know My Word and be sensitive to My Spirit to know what My thoughts are. Three weapons to pull down strongholds are 1) My Word 2) My blood shed on the cross and 3) My name, Jesus. Use these weapons and strongholds will be pulled down and bondages will be broken.

Father, I declare I know Your Word and I cast down all arguments and every high and prideful thing that exalts itself against You. I bring every thought into captivity to the obedience of You. In Jesus' name Amen.

NOTES:

ೀೀೀೀೀೀೀೀೀೀೀೀೀೀೀೀೀೀೀೀೀೀೀೀೀ

WEEK 21
❖JESUS THE HIGH PRIEST❖

ೀೀೀೀೀೀೀೀೀೀೀೀೀೀೀೀೀೀೀೀೀೀೀೀೀ

DAY 1
Read Hebrews 4:14-5:10; Hebrews 7:15-28

I am your High Priest. I am the kind of High Priest you need because I am holy and blameless, unstained by sin. I have been set apart from sinners and given the highest place of honor in heaven (Hebrews 7:26).

In the Old Testament the High Priest of Israel passed through the courts and veils into the Most Holy Place. I, Jesus, your High Priest have passed through the heavens to the very presence of our Father God, where I sit at our Father God's right hand. I am a compassionate High Priest, loving and caring.

Father, thank You for Jesus my loving and compassionate High Priest, who sits at Your right hand. In Jesus' name Amen.

ೀೀೀೀೀೀೀೀೀೀೀ

DAY 2
Read Hebrews 4:14-5:10; Hebrews 7:15-28

I am a High Priest who understands your weaknesses because I faced all the same temptations as you but without sinning. I will help you to not sin when tempted if you will only ask Me. I am there for you

Everyone is tempted. Being tempted is not sin but giving in to the temptation is sin. I can help you overcome.

Father, thank You for giving me Jesus who can sympathize with me and will help me have victory over temptations. In Jesus' name Amen.

DAY 3
Read Hebrews 4:14-5:10; Hebrews 7:15-28

Since I am a High Priest who was tempted in all ways as you were without sin and I can sympathize with you and have compassion on you, you can boldly come to our Father's throne and find mercy and grace in your time of need.

It is because of My work on the cross that you can boldly, fearlessly and with great confidence approach our Father's presence because He is full of grace and I, your High Priest, sit at His right hand interceding for you.

Father, thank You that I can boldly and confidently come to Your throne of grace and find mercy. In Jesus' name Amen.

DAY 4
Read Hebrews 4:14-5:10; Hebrews 7:15-28

Because of Me and My shed blood on the cross and your faith in Me, you can now come boldly and confidently into our Father's presence (Ephesians 3:12; Hebrews 10:19-22).

You are clean and have been washed by My blood. You don't have to be fearful approaching our Father. He loves you and wants to fellowship with you.

Father, I declare I have faith and confidence to approach You. I come boldly to Your throne. In Jesus' name Amen.

❧❧❧❧❧❧❧❧❧❧❧❧

DAY 5
Read Hebrews 4:14-5:10; Hebrews 7:15-28

I want you to understand that I am your High Priest (Jesus) and I intercede for you to our Father as you boldly come to My throne. I am sitting at the right hand of our Father and He loves to hear from you and loves to bless you.

You will find mercy and grace in our Father's presence. What do I mean by mercy and grace? Mercy means blessings of forgiveness and compassion; withholding of the punishment or judgment your sins deserve. Grace is My favor. You are righteous through My blood. Our Father sees you as righteous so boldly come.

Thank You, Father, for Jesus as my High Priest that has mercy on me as I come to You. I come to You Father, in Jesus' name and praise You.

❧❧❧❧❧❧❧❧❧❧❧❧

DAY 6
Read Hebrews 4:14-5:10; Hebrews 7:15-28

I want you to know you can boldly come into My presence and find love, compassion and My favor which is love, kindness, approval, and blessings.

I am proud of you and hold nothing from you. You don't have to be fearful of Me. I am here for you and want to bestow blessings upon you but you have to be willing to receive My blessings and be confident of My love and My favor.

Father, I declare that I have Your love, mercy and grace as I come into Your presence. I will not fear but will come boldly into Your presence and willingly receive Your blessings. In Jesus name Amen

Read Hebrews 4:14-5:10; Hebrews 7:15-28

Regarding prayer, these passages are important for you to know. You need to know that I am your High Priest who sympathizes with you. I know what it's like to be tempted but without sinning. I can help you overcome temptation without sinning.

I have love and compassion for you. You can boldly come into My presence and I will give you grace and mercy. Come into My presence, I love you. I am always here for you. My arms are open wide to receive you no matter what. I want to pour out blessings on you.

Father, I declare You are my High Priest who can sympathize with me and can show me how to overcome temptation and not sin. Thank You for Your love and compassion for me and giving me grace and mercy. I love You, Father. In Jesus' name Amen.

NOTES:

つつつつつつつつつつつつつつつつつつつ

WEEK 22
❖DON'T WORRY, PRAY❖

つつつつつつつつつつつつつつつつつつ

DAY 1
Read Philippians 4:6-7; 1 Peter 5:7

You are not to worry about anything instead pray about everything. Worry is a preoccupation with things causing anxiety, stress, and pressure. Worry and anxiety are not of Me. If you are worrying, you are not focused on Me or walking in faith.

I am ever mindful of your daily needs (Matthew 6:25-34). Worry is a sin and has never changed a thing other than your health and peace of mind.

Father, I am sorry for the times I have worried over things. I surrender all to You because I know You will take care of everything I need. Thank You Lord. In Jesus' name Amen.

つつつつつつつつつつ

DAY 2
Read Philippians 4:6-7; 1 Peter 5:7

When you are worrying you are not walking in faith. When you worry, you're walking in fear which is the opposite of faith. I have not given you a spirit of fear, but of power, love and a sound mind. Remember, you cannot please Me without faith. Instead of worrying pray about everything.

Give all your worries and cares to Me, for I care for you. If you acknowledge Me in all things I will direct your path (Proverbs 3:6). When you worry, you open the door to the devil and he will bring about what you are worrying about.

Father, I cast all my cares and worries on You. I know You care about me and watch over me. Thank You, Father. In Jesus' name Amen.

DAY 3
Read Philippians 4:6-7; 1 Peter 5:7

You are to pray about everything with thanksgiving. You need to come to Me with a grateful heart not a complaining or critical heart. You are to be thankful in all circumstances (I Thessalonians 5:18).

It doesn't say to be thankful <u>for</u> all circumstances but to be thankful <u>in</u> all circumstances. You can be thankful in the midst of bad things because you know I am with you and I will see you through any and all trials.

Father, Thank You for Your love and mercy and for sending Jesus to die for me. I declare I will have a grateful heart in and through all circumstances knowing You will see me through every trial I face. In Jesus' name Amen.

DAY 4
Read Philippians 4:6-7; 1 Peter 5:7

You are to pray with thanksgiving and continue to make your requests known to Me. I know you are wondering why you need to continue to make your requests known to Me when I already know what you need and want? It is because I want you to know you can come to Me with anything and I will listen and answer your prayers. I am a good Father and love you and want to fellowship with you.

As a parent, you know what your children need and want but you like them to come talk with you about those things. I am the same. I want you to come to Me in times of struggle as well as the good times and talk to Me and ask Me for anything.

Father, I declare I can come to You with anything and You will hear and answer my requests. I come to You with thanksgiving in my heart. In Jesus' name Amen.

৵৵৵৵৵৵৵৵৵৵৵

DAY 5
Read Philippians 4:6-7; 1 Peter 5:7

My peace which passes all understanding is a state of rest, quietness and calmness; an absence of strife. It is tranquility, completeness, wholeness, health, welfare, safety, soundness, prosperity, perfectness, fullness, and harmony, the absence of agitation or discord.

I want you to live with this peace but you must not worry and must seek Me. When you do, you will have this peace in your life.

Father, I declare I will not have worry and anxiety in my life. I will have Your peace as I acknowledge You in all things and have a thankful heart. In Jesus' name Amen.

৵৵৵৵৵৵৵৵৵৵৵

DAY 6
Read Philippians 4:6-7; 1 Peter 5:7

You can have My peace that passes all understanding. To get it you must not worry and must pray about everything with thanksgiving. You are to praise Me and be thankful and you will have My peace.

My peace will guard your heart and your mind. Rejoice in Me. My joy will give you strength and peace of mind.

Father, Thank You for Your peace that passes all understanding. I declare I will not worry but pray about every circumstance with thanksgiving and experience Your wonderful presence and peace. In Jesus' name Amen.

DAY 7 - SUMMARY
Read Philippians 4:6-7; 1 Peter 5:7

Pray always with thanksgiving and do not worry or fret over things. I will give you My peace that passes understanding. I love you and want to give you My peace.

I want you to trust me with all things and have a grateful heart. I know and understand all you are going through. Continue to make your wants known to Me and you will have My peace.

Father, I declare I come to You with thanksgiving and I will not fret over things. I have Your peace that passes all understanding. When I am in peace, I won't understand it but I will know You have given it to me. In Jesus' name Amen.

NOTES:

≈≈≈≈≈≈≈≈≈≈≈≈≈≈≈≈≈≈≈≈≈≈≈

WEEK 23
❖GOD SOUGHT A MAN❖

≈≈≈≈≈≈≈≈≈≈≈≈≈≈≈≈≈≈≈≈≈≈≈

DAY 1
Read Ezekiel 22:30-31; Exodus 32:9-11

The Israelites in these verses refused to answer My call to intercede so I wouldn't have to destroy the land. Even Ezekiel couldn't lead them. A qualified leader is useless if people refuse to be led.

You may think that just one person can't make a difference but I sought a man (person). I wasn't seeking a group of people but only one person to stand in the gap. That one person could've gotten the job done just like Moses interceding for the Israelites.

Father, I answer Your call to stand in the gap for Your people and for those that are lost and can't find their way. Thank You, Lord, for giving me the opportunity to stand in the gap. In Jesus' name Amen.

≈≈≈≈≈≈≈≈≈≈≈

DAY 2
Read Ezekiel 22:30-31; Exodus 32:9-11

Moses (just himself) stood in the gap for the Israelites. I was mad at the Israelites for building the golden calf and worshipping it. I told Moses to leave Me alone so I could consume them…but Moses wouldn't leave Me alone. He interceded for the nation. I relented from the harm which I said I would do to My people.

So you see by this passage your prayers are very important and there's many more standing in the gap today than just one.

Father, thank You for hearing me whether I am praying by myself or there are many, You always answer. I answer Your call to pray and intercede whatever is on Your heart, Lord. In Jesus' name Amen.

DAY 3
Read Ezekiel 22:30-31; Exodus 32:9-11

Abraham stood in the gap for Sodom and Gomorrah in Genesis 18. I was about to pour out judgment on Sodom and Gomorrah. Because Abraham was My friend, I told him what I planned to do. Abraham asked Me repeatedly to spare them for the sake of the righteous and I granted his every request. He quit too soon but I sent angels to escort his family out of Sodom and Gomorrah before judgment fell.

Are you a friend of Mine? Is your relationship with Me close enough for Me to tell you what I am planning to do giving you the opportunity to pray for that situation?

As My born again child, you should have that closeness so that I will let you in on what's going to happen and trust you to pray about it. My Spirit will tell you things to come (John 16:13) but I have given you the responsibility and authority to intercede about those things.

Father, I declare that I am Your friend and You can trust me with telling me things to come to pray about and intercede for. Thank You for the opportunity to stand in the gap. In Jesus' name Amen.

DAY 4
Read Ezekiel 22:30-31; Exodus 32:9-11

I am seeking people to stand in the gap, to pray and to intercede. Answer My call.

I have made it clear from Genesis to Revelation that prayer is the match that lights the fuse to release the explosive power of My Spirit in the affairs of your life. Give prayer priority time.

Father, I declare I give prayer priority time in my life as You call me to intercede. In Jesus' name Amen.

DAY 5
Read Ezekiel 22:30-31; Exodus 32:9-11

I found no one to stand in the gap, no one to build up the wall or intercede for the land that I should not destroy it. You are My representative on the earth and need to be a living sacrifice (Romans 12:1) for Me.

Sometimes you wonder why I don't intervene in things. You say I could've stopped something or caused something to happen but maybe no one was praying.

I have set up laws and principles that I abide by. I have given you everything you need for life and Godliness (2 Peter 1:2-4). You need to take the responsibility and authority I have given you and be My representative on the earth.

Father, I don't want You to ever say You couldn't find someone to stand in the gap. I declare I am Your representative on the earth and take my responsibility and authority and pray and intercede on the earth as the Spirit leads. In Jesus' name Amen.

DAY 6
Read Ezekiel 22:30-31; Exodus 32:9-11

I poured out My indignation upon the city and consumed them with the fire of My wrath just because I couldn't find anyone to stand in the gap.

Answer the call to stand in the gap so you can keep the devil out of My people and their lives and your life. I give you the power and authority and responsibility.

Father, I declare I will stand in the gap for my brothers and sisters in Christ and for the lost that they will have an encounter with You. In Jesus' name Amen.

ひひひひひひひひひひ

DAY 7 - SUMMARY
Read Ezekiel 22:30-31; Exodus 32:9-11

These verses are a call to prayer. I sought a man to stand in the gap but I couldn't find anyone and had to destroy the land. I am still seeking those who will stand in the gap for My people and the lost.

Moses stood in the gap for the Israelites and Abraham stood in the gap for Sodom and Gomorrah. Many others in My Word stood in the gap for My people. Answer that call and stand in the gap for others.

Father, I answer Your call to stand in the gap for others and seek the Spirit's leading to know what to pray. In Jesus' name Amen.

NOTES:

òòòòòòòòòòòòòòòòòòòòòòò
WEEK 24
❖WATCHMAN ON THE WALL❖
òòòòòòòòòòòòòòòòòòòòòòò

DAY 1
Read Isaiah 62:6-7

Watchmen on the wall are those who look out, peer into the distance, and keep watch for approaching danger. In the Old Testament, they used watchmen on their walls to keep an eye on who comes and goes and for any danger. When they saw someone approaching, they sounded the shofar or yelled it out.

In other instances it is spiritual watchmen, or prophets who lookout, see danger, and report to the people. That's what the prophets in the Old Testament did.

Father, I declare I am a watchman on the wall to sound the alarm of danger. In Jesus' name Amen.

òòòòòòòòòòò

DAY 2
Read Isaiah 62:6-7

An intercessor is called a watchman on the wall because an intercessor is being alert and listening for the leading of My Spirit and watching for danger from the enemy.

You are to be vigilant, keenly watchful to detect danger, ever awake and alert and cautious at all times because your enemy, the devil, roams around like a lion seeking someone to devour (1Peter 5:8-9). You are to withstand him. I have given you the power and authority to stand against him in My name.

Adam was to be a watchman in the Garden of Eden. I told him to keep the garden which meant to protect and preserve it but he failed and Satan took over (Genesis 2:15).

Father, I declare I am alert and watchful for the devil and his dirty tricks and schemes. I will resist him. In Jesus' name Amen.

DAY 3
Read Isaiah 62:6-7

You are to be watchmen for Israel, My people. You are to pray for the peace of Jerusalem and stand in the gap for them (Psalm 122:6).

Pray day and night, continually. Give Me no rest until the work is done and Jerusalem is the pride of the earth. You will be blessed as you stand in the gap.

Father, I declare I will be a watchman on the wall for Israel and stand in the gap for them. In Jesus' name Amen.

DAY 4
Read Isaiah 62:6-7

It is important that you pray for Israel but you are watchmen on the wall for whatever or whoever My Spirit leads you to pray for.

My Spirit will show you things to come that you should stand in the gap for (John 16:13). You must stay alert and be watchful and intercede as I lead. My Spirit is in you leading you.

Father, I declare I am alert and watchful for whatever or whoever You want me to pray for. Thank You, Lord, for the opportunity to stand in the gap. In Jesus' name Amen.

DAY 5
Read Isaiah 62:6-7

As watchmen, you are not to keep silent. You are to put Me in remembrance of My promises. Of course, I don't forget my promises but I like you to speak My Word to Me and as you do I will answer. My Word will not return void (Isaiah 55:11).

As watchmen, you need to keep alert of the devil's schemes. You are not to be ignorant of his wiles and intentions (2 Corinthians 2:11). My Spirit will warn or alert you of the devil's schemes if you will be sensitive and alert.

Father, I declare I am watchful and alert to the schemes of the devil and take my place as an intercessor and stop him before he attacks. In Jesus' name Amen.

DAY 6
Read Isaiah 62:6-7

You are to not just be watchmen on the wall for Israel, America, or whatever I put on your heart but you are to also watch over your heart with all diligence for from it flow the springs of life (Proverbs 4:23).

You must guard what you allow to enter into your heart, if you don't Satan will succeed in establishing strongholds in you. What you allow in your heart and mind, will come out of your mouth (Matthew 12:34; 15:18-19; Luke 6:45).

Father, I declare I will watch and guard over my heart with all diligence and only allow good things in my heart and speak only good things. In Jesus' name Amen.

DAY 7 - SUMMARY
Read Isaiah 62:6-7

I am calling you to be a watchman on the wall, to be alert to the enemy's schemes. You are to warn of his tactics and intercede. I give you the authority to resist the enemy.

You must know your enemy and his schemes to know how and what to pray for. You need to also watch over your heart and not allow anything that is not of Me to enter.

Thank You, Father, for the opportunity to be a watchman on the wall. I will take my position and stand in the gap. In Jesus' name Amen.

NOTES:

WEEK 25
❖GOD HEARS YOU❖

DAY 1
Read Psalm 34:4-10, 15-18; Psalm 66:19; 2 Chronicles 15:2

It is important to seek Me first and I will be there. As born again believers, I am always there because the Spirit dwells within you but you still need to seek Me first (Matthew 6:33).

As you do, I will answer you and free you from all your fears and you will be radiant with joy. My joy gives you strength.

Father, I seek You first in all things and as I do I find You and You answer. Thank You, Lord. In Jesus' name Amen.

DAY 2
Read Psalm 34:4-10, 15-18; Psalm 66:19; 2 Chronicles 15:2

When you seek Me, I will deliver you from all your fears. "All" means "all"; from all of your fears. I will deliver you from "all" your troubles.

You just need to seek Me and cry out to Me and I will hear you and you will be delivered. I am always there for you. I will never leave you or forsake you.

You just need to trust Me, seek Me and I will save you from all your fears and troubles.

Thank You, Father, for saving me from all my fears and troubles as I seek You and cry out to You. You hear me and answer. In Jesus' name Amen.

ഏഏഏഏഏഏഏഏഏഏ

DAY 3
Read Psalm 34:4-10, 15-18; Psalm 66:19; 2 Chronicles 15:2

As My children, you all have angels that encamp around you and minister to you (Hebrews 1:14). If you fear and reverence Me, My angels will surround and defend and deliver you.

I hear you when you seek Me and cry out to Me. I deliver you by sending My angels to surround you. Never stop seeking Me.

Thank You, Father, for your angels that surround me, guard and deliver me. In Jesus' name Amen.

ഏഏഏഏഏഏഏഏഏഏ

DAY 4
Read Psalm 34:4-10, 15-18; Psalm 66:19; 2 Chronicles 15:2

When you seek Me by My Word, you are feeding on or tasting My Word; evaluating it and discerning it. You come to know Me and My goodness by meditating on My Word and seeking My presence and perceive My goodness.

You are blessed when you take refuge in Me and trust Me. Fear (reverence and worship) Me and you will have all you need. Those who trust Me will lack no beneficial thing.

Father, I taste and see that You are good. I will be blessed as I trust You and take refuge in You. I worship You and reverence You and declare I have no lack in any beneficial thing as long as I seek You. In Jesus' name Amen.

శ్రీశ్రీశ్రీశ్రీశ్రీశ్రీ

DAY 5
Read Psalm 34:4-10, 15-18; Psalm 66:19; 2 Chronicles 15:2

I hear and pay attention to those who seek Me. I hear you. I have given heed to the voice of your prayers (Psalm 17:1; 55:2; 61:1; 86:6; 130:2; 142:6).

In the same way that My eyes roam to and fro throughout the earth, seeking those whose hearts are truly Mine (see 2 Chronicles 16:9), My ears are always listening for the voices of My children. I am all ears. Seek Me and call out to Me and I will deliver you from all your fears.

Father, I thank You that You hear my prayers and You answer me. You are always listening for me. In Jesus' name Amen.

శ్రీశ్రీశ్రీశ్రీశ్రీశ్రీ

DAY 6
Read Psalm 34:4-10, 15-18; Psalm 66:19; 2 Chronicles 15:2

I am eavesdropping on you, waiting for you to speak to Me. I just can't wait for you to come to me.

It's important for you to be attentive to Me as I am with you. Prayer is dialogue not monologue. I am available any time. Let's have a conversation. I am waiting to hear from you.

Father, You are always attentive to what I am saying, whether I am speaking to You or to others. Help me to be as attentive to You as You are to me. In Jesus' name Amen.

❧❧❧❧❧❧❧❧❧❧

DAY 7 - SUMMARY
Read Psalm 34:4-10, 15-18; Psalm 66:19; 2 Chronicles 15:2

Most of Psalm 34 is about Me hearing you when you seek Me, when you cry out to Me and I will deliver you from all of your fears. I am attentive to you. I see you. You can't hide from Me. I see you and know what you are doing and hear everything you say whether speaking to Me or to others or speaking to yourself.

You need to be attentive to Me and hear what I am saying to you. I am always hearing you and speaking to you either through My Word, through other people, or a strong witness in your spirit. I don't usually speak audibly to you but I could but it would be like a whisper (1 Kings 19:11-12). Always be listening and obeying Me.

Father, thank You for hearing my prayers and answering. I declare I have ears to hear what You are saying to me and I will be obedient to Your Word. In Jesus' name Amen.

NOTES:

DAY 5
Read Psalm 34:1-3; 1 Thessalonians 5:18
Psalm 147:5; Hebrews 13:15

You are to constantly and at all times offer up a sacrifice of praise. What is that sacrifice? It is the fruit of lips with thanksgiving. Why is praising Me a sacrifice? Praise often requires that you "kill" your pride, fear, laziness, or flesh-anything that threatens to diminish or interfere with your worship of Me.

Sacrifice in English sometimes suggests just an inconvenience or the giving of a costly gift.

In Hebrew it involves the offering of a life which you are offering your life to Me when you worship Me. You are to be a living sacrifice (Romans 12:1).

Father, I declare I am a living sacrifice to You and will praise and worship You continually. In Jesus' name Amen.

DAY 6
Read Psalm 34:1-3; 1 Thessalonians 5:18
Psalm 147:5; Hebrews 13:15

You are to encourage others to praise and worship Me and to tell others of My greatness. You are to exalt My name together with others in unity.

I am worthy of your praise and I will hear your prayers and deliver you from all your fears and troubles.

Father, I want to praise and worship You continually and encourage others to praise You because You are a great God and worthy to be praised. In Jesus' name Amen.

DAY 7 - SUMMARY
Read Psalm 34:1-3; 1 Thessalonians 5:18
Psalm 147:5; Hebrews 13:15

You need to continually praise and worship Me. You should start your prayers with praise and worship because I am worthy of your praises.

You are to come to Me with grateful hearts giving Me praise and thanksgiving. When you do, I will hear you and deliver you from all your fears and trials. You are to be a living sacrifice. Sometimes praise and thanksgiving to Me is a sacrifice.

I thank You, Father, for Your goodness and grace on my life. I declare I praise and worship You continually with a grateful heart. Thank You, Father. I love You and praise Your Holy name. In Jesus' name Amen.

NOTES:

≈≈≈≈≈≈≈≈≈≈≈≈≈≈≈≈≈≈≈≈≈≈≈≈

WEEK 27
❖THE GOOD SHEPHERD❖

≈≈≈≈≈≈≈≈≈≈≈≈≈≈≈≈≈≈≈≈≈≈≈≈

DAY 1
Read John 10:1-17; Psalm 23:2-3

I am your good Shepherd and you are My sheep. I know your name and call you out. You are to listen to My voice and heed it. Listen for My voice as I call out to you.

You know My voice and follow Me. Do not follow a stranger. A stranger will guide you in the wrong direction so run away from a stranger.

Father, I declare I listen for Your voice and heed it as You call out my name. In Jesus' name Amen.

DAY 2
Read John 10:1-17; Psalm 23:2-3

I am up close and personal with you. I know your name and know you personally (read Psalm 139). I am calling your name. Listen and answer that call. Do not get away from Me.

When sheep get away from the shepherd and the other sheep, it puts itself in danger of being devoured by the enemy. Do not be a lone ranger, thinking you don't need to be in a church with other believers. Watching TV ministers or church on the internet is ok once in a while but you need the fellowship of other believers.

Father, thank You for calling me by name and taking care of me as the Good Shepherd. In Jesus' name Amen.

DAY 3
Read John 10:1-17; Psalm 23:2-3

I will not drive you or push you. You are not like cattle, which have to be driven. That's why it's called a cattle drive when they are taking them somewhere.

I will direct, supervise and influence you as you listen to My voice and follow Me. In leading you, I am always ahead as you follow. If you get ahead of Me, you are no longer listening or following Me. To follow Me is pursuing, seeking, or running after Me; imitating Me and obeying Me. Keep seeking and listening for My leading and be obedient.

I want you to know that if you will listen and obey My voice, I will always be for you, never against you. Do not rebel against My Word. Follow after Me. I'm all you need. I love you, My Child. Never doubt My love. I am love and want to comfort you, heal you, and set you free from all of your fears. Just trust Me, listen and obey.

Father, thank You for leading me to the still and restful water. I declare I am listening for Your voice, following after You and being obedient. In Jesus' name Amen.

DAY 4
Read John 10:1-17; Psalm 23:2-3

I will walk ahead of you and you will follow Me because you are My child and you know My voice.

Sometimes I speak through My Word, so you need to be reading My Word to know Me and know My voice. Sometimes I speak through other people and most of the time it is just an inner witness, My Holy Spirit speaking to your spirit. I don't usually speak loudly, but in a whisper (I Kings 19:11-12).

Father, I declare I know Your voice and I follow You and obey You. In Jesus' name Amen.

DAY 5
Read John 10:1-17; Psalm 23:2-3

You should never follow a stranger but run away from him because you do not know the voice of strangers. You are so close to Me and know My voice, you recognize My voice only.

You need to be so intimate with Me that you recognize My voice and follow Me only. Since you recognize My voice and follow Me, you will not be deceived and swayed to the way of the world. If you stay in My Word, there will be less chance of being deceived or swayed away from Me.

Father, I want to know You intimately and know Your voice that I will not follow a stranger's voice. In Jesus' name Amen.

DAY 6
Read John 10:1-17; Psalm 23:2-3

There are three voices that you hear from within. The three voices you listen to all the time are: My voice; the voices of Satan or evil spirits; and self-talk; your own inner talk. I always speak lovingly, gently, peacefully, and never push and I am never negative. I am your advocate, your comforter and will never leave you.

The voices of Satan and evil spirits are negative, always putting doubt in your mind. Satan's favorite words are always, "things are always going to be this bad", never: "you will never be able to change" or "God will never love you after what you have done."

Self-talk is the voice of your flesh. You should be talking and confessing My Word in self-talk so if you are not, do not listen to yourself. If you listen to yourself, you will be defeated because it's mostly from what you hear from things around you in the world, from TV and worldly teaching. Get into My Word and talk what My Word says, declare My word into your life and you will be able to hear My voice and have victory in your life.

Father, I declare I will listen only to Your voice, Your Word and not listen to the words of the devil or self-talk that is influenced by the world. In Jesus' name Amen.

ﾟﾟﾟﾟﾟﾟﾟﾟﾟﾟﾟﾟ

DAY 7 - SUMMARY
Read John 10:1-17; Psalm 23:2-3

I AM your Shepherd and you are My child, you are My sheep. You are to listen to My voice and heed it. I will lead you and you are to follow. You are to be intimate with Me, your Shepherd and know My voice. A stranger's voice you recognize as a stranger and run from it.

I know you and call you by name. I never push you but gently lead you. Every believer can and does hear My voice. My Spirit dwells within you and will always be there leading you and speaking to you.

Father, I thank You for being my Shepherd. I will heed Your voice and follow after You. I want to know You more and be intimate with You. In Jesus name Amen.

NOTES:

ৡৡৡৡৡৡৡৡৡৡৡৡৡৡৡৡৡৡৡৡৡৡৡৡৡৡ

WEEK 28
❖ASK FOR GOD'S WISDOM❖

ৡৡৡৡৡৡৡৡৡৡৡৡৡৡৡৡৡৡৡৡৡৡৡৡৡৡ

DAY 1
Read James 1:5-8

Just because you think you have worldly wisdom, My wisdom is what matters most. My wisdom is insight and revelation into spiritual things. I want to give you this wisdom and you will have a successful life.

Proverbs says that reverent and worshipful fear of Me is the beginning of wisdom (Proverbs 1:7). To fear Me isn't being afraid of Me but to reverence or respect Me as the Lord, and to be in awe of Me.

Father, I declare I have Your wisdom not the wisdom of the world. I worshipfully and reverently fear You and stand in awe of You. In Jesus' name Amen.

DAY 2
Read James 1:5-8

You are to seek wisdom, insight and understanding as hidden treasure (Proverbs 2:3-6). I will grant you this wisdom if you ask for it. I will give it to you liberally, without rebuke.

Wisdom from Me is pure, peaceable, and gentle, willing to yield to reason, full of mercy and good fruits. It shows no favoritism and is always sincere (James 3:17). My wisdom is the wisdom you should be seeking, not the wisdom of the world that tries to get ahead and successful at all costs.

Father, I ask You for this wisdom from above. I reverently fear You and I declare I have this wisdom You desire to give me. Thank You. In Jesus' name Amen.

DAY 3
Read James 1:5-8

I will grant you this wisdom if you ask Me but you must ask in faith. It is impossible to please Me without faith (Hebrews 11:6). You have to believe that I exist and that I am the rewarder of those who diligently seek Me.

If you are praying but have no faith, you are wasting your breath and My time because I will not hear your prayer. If you are struggling to get an answer from Me about something, check your faith and how you are praying.

Father, I declare I will come to You in faith and with the right motive and ask for the things on my heart. I want to please You. In Jesus' name Amen.

DAY 4
Read James 1:5-8

Asking Me in faith and with the right motive is the only way to get your prayers answered. You will not receive from Me if you ask with the wrong motive and want only what will give you pleasure (James 4:3).

Check your faith and motives when you are praying and asking Me for things in your life.

Father, I declare my faith and motives are right as I come to You in prayer. In Jesus' name Amen.

DAY 5
Read James 1:5-8

It must be in faith that you ask me with no wavering (no hesitating, not doubting). You are in doubt about many things. You can tell when you are in doubt when you pray one thing and turn around and say something else.

For example, you pray for healing and confess the Scriptures about healing and say you believe and receive it and then five minutes after praying and confessing you are complaining about how bad you feel. You just wiped out the prayer and confession you just made.

That is being double-minded and wavering which is doubting, being in indecision and hesitating in your faith. Wavering is like the billowing surge of the sea, with high waves tossed by the wind. You cannot pray in doubt and expect an answer from Me. Remember, it is impossible to please Me without faith.

Father, I declare I will not doubt and be double-minded when I pray. I know You will hear me and answer when I pray in faith. In Jesus' name Amen.

DAY 6
Read James 1:5-8

Being double-minded is being of two minds, one in the world and one in the spiritual. If you are double-minded, you are unstable and unreliable and uncertain about everything.

To be of one mind you must get into My Word, study and meditate on it. If you are indecisive about something, find Scriptures about that issue and confess them rather than the problem. I will not answer your prayers if you are double-minded because you are not in faith.

Father, I declare I am of one mind which is set on You and I come to You in faith, not wavering. In Jesus' name Amen.

DAY 7 - SUMMARY
Read James 1:5-8

If you are deficient in wisdom, you can ask Me and I will be happy to give it to you in abundance. To ask for it, you must be in faith no wavering or doubting. If you are in doubt, you are double-minded and unstable and will not receive from Me because without faith it is impossible to please Me.

This faith is My finished work on the cross. Your faith is in and generated in that finished work. I have given you access to God our Father. That is your faith and confidence in Me.

If you have doubts about something, get into My Word, study and meditate on it and your faith will increase.

Father, I ask for Your wisdom and I come to You in faith, not doubting or wavering. Thank You for Your wisdom. In Jesus' name Amen.

NOTES:

WEEK 29
❖DON'T PRAY LIKE THE HYPOCRITES❖

DAY 1
Read Matthew 6:5-8; Psalm 91:1

I am not against public prayer. In fact, I call My people to corporate prayer. I am against public prayer that attracts attention to those people and those wanting the approval of man rather than My approval. These people have received their reward already and will not receive anything from Me.

A hypocrite is a person who portrays a false appearance of religion or who acts in contradiction to his or her stated beliefs and who pretend to be something else than what they really are.

Father, I will not be a hypocrite when I pray. I will not look at other's who may be hypocrites but will focus on You only and glorify You in my prayers. In Jesus' name Amen.

DAY 2
Read Matthew 6:5-8; Psalm 91:1

You do need to go away by yourself, shut the door behind you and pray to Me in private. I am waiting for you. I am listening for you.

Time with Me is important and precious for your relationship with Me. If you have trouble finding time, ask Me and I will help you. If you are serious about Me helping you find time with Me, I can rearrange things for you. I can cause the neighbor to have to rev his truck up to keep it going in the morning to wake you up and get you in the habit. Nothing is impossible for Me. I enjoy spending time with you and will do whatever needs to be done to allow you to find that time.

Father, I declare that I will find a place and time to come and spend quiet time with You. Thank You for helping me. In Jesus' name Amen.

DAY 3
Read Matthew 6:5-8; Psalm 91:1

When you spend quiet time with Me, I will reward you. I am in secret and I see in secret.

If you want to remain stable and fixed under My shadow, you need to come to that secret place by finding time with Me and you will remain stable and I will reward you. My presence is all you need.

Father, I declare I will find time to come to You and dwell in the secret place and be in Your presence. I will remain stable and You will reward me openly. In Jesus' name Amen.

DAY 4
Read Matthew 6:5-8; Psalm 91:1

The secret place is dwelling in My presence. I want every one of My children to dwell in the secret place under My shadow. I want to protect you and keep you safe from the evil in the world but you need to stay close to Me.

When you are in the secret place, be sure to listen more. Tune out those thoughts that bring you doubts and foolish things that have nothing to do with anything.

I am the vine, you are the branches, you must remain in Me to produce fruit (John 15:1-8). You need to dwell in Me and I will dwell in you. You must remain connected to Me at all times. Without Me you can do nothing.

Father, I declare that I dwell in the secret place, in Your presence. I will stay connected to You. In Jesus' name Amen.

DAY 5
Read Matthew 6:5-8; Psalm 91:1

Verse 7 of Matthew 6 in the NLT says don't babble on and on. Babble means to talk idly, irrationally, excessively or foolishly; chatter or prattle. (Read I Kings 18:26). In the NKJV it says vain repetition; the Amplified says, don't heap up phrases (multiplying words, repeating the same one over and over). It's ok to repeat a request and other prayers such as The Lord's Prayer but don't do it mindlessly.

Some people just repeat prayers but it's not from their hearts. I won't honor those prayers. I look at the heart. I want you to pray My Word and confess My Word over your lives and situations. You don't need to pray long drawn out prayers. My prayers were short and to the point. Most of the time, I didn't pray for others, I just spoke and it was done. You are to do the same.

Father, I declare my prayers are short and to the point. I will not babble on and on. In Jesus' name Amen.

DAY 6
Read Matthew 6:5-8; Psalm 91:1

You are not to pray meaningless prayers for I know exactly what you need before you ask Me. This is repeated several different times in Scriptures (Matthew 6:32; Luke 12:30; 1 John 3:20). I'm sure many are asking, "If I already know what you need why do you need to pray?" Anyone who has children should know the answer to that question. You desire your children to come to you and ask for things and talk to you, even though you know what they may need. That is how you develop a relationship with them.

I am no different. I know you and know all you need but I desire fellowship with you and enjoy your company and talking with you. Prayer is just communicating to Me and Me to you. I love you and desire a close relationship with you.

Father, I desire a close relationship with You and will seek Your presence and talk with You. In Jesus' name Amen.

Read Matthew 6:5-8; Psalm 91:1

You are not to be hypocrites in your praying. You are not to pray to get the approval of others. My approval is all you need. You need to find a quiet time to be with Me. I love your company and will reward you when you seek Me. Come to the secret place, dwelling in My presence.

You are to talk to Me as you would another person, don't babble on and on, begging or being dishonorable with many words. I know exactly what you need but desire you coming to Me, asking and fellowshipping with Me.

Father, I declare I will not pray to get man's approval but Yours only. I will find quiet time to be in Your presence, in the secret place. I will not babble on and on and speak mindlessly to You. I love You Lord. In Jesus' name Amen.

NOTES:

ༀༀༀༀༀༀༀༀༀༀༀༀༀༀༀༀༀༀༀༀༀༀༀༀ

WEEK 30
❖THE LORD'S PRAYER❖

ༀༀༀༀༀༀༀༀༀༀༀༀༀༀༀༀༀༀༀༀༀༀༀༀ

DAY 1
Read Matthew 6:9-14

The disciples asked Me to teach them to pray. I gave this prayer as an example of what to pray for not as a prayer to repeat every day. You should start your prayers with praise and worship to Me. "Father" is a note of personal intimacy. You are to call God Father, Abba Father (Romans 8:15). You are My children. I am your Abba Father. Come to Me with praise and worship.

Abba, Daddy, I love You and praise You because You are worthy of my praise. In Jesus' name Amen.

DAY 2
Read Matthew 6:9-14

You are to pray for My Kingdom to come and reign on the earth and My will be done on earth as it is in heaven. There is no sickness, no lack, no evil, no depression or infirmity in heaven.

My will is that you are healed, prosperous, in peace, delivered and set free from evil. I have provided these things on the cross; you just need to learn how to receive all I have provided (Read Isaiah 53).

Father, I pray Your Kingdom come. I declare Your will be done on earth and in my life as it is in heaven. In Jesus' name Amen.

DAY 3
Read Matthew 6:9-14

You are to pray for daily provision which I will provide. You are My child and I will take care of you even if you don't ask daily. You should thank Me daily for your provision.

I am a good, good Father and I take care of My children. I meet your needs according to My riches in glory (Philippians 4:19).

Father, Thank You for giving me food on the table, a roof over my head, clothes on my body and money to pay my bills. You are my provider and a good, good Father. In Jesus' name Amen.

DAY 4
Read Matthew 6:9-14

It is important to forgive others as I have forgiven you. Un-forgiveness will affect you in many ways but mainly affects your relationship with Me. Because I expect you to forgive, I will help you when you ask Me. I cannot forgive you, if you do not forgive others.

Father, thank You for forgiving me of all my sins. I declare I will walk in love and forgiveness toward others. In Jesus' name Amen.

DAY 5
Read Matthew 6:9-14

I do not lead you into temptation. The devil is the one who puts temptation in your path. The devil comes to steal, kill and destroy. I give life abundantly (John 10:10).

I will rescue you from the evil one. Temptation is not sin but if you give into it that is the sin.

Father, I declare I will not yield to temptation and I declare You will deliver me from the evil one. In Jesus' name Amen.

DAY 6
Read Matthew 6:9-14

The last of this prayer is praise and worship again. So you need to start your prayer with praise, worship, and thanksgiving and end prayer with praise, worship and thanksgiving. Sandwiched in between is the petition, supplications and intercession.

You need to remember this prayer by Me was given before My death and resurrection. I said in John 16:23-24 that you are to pray in My name but you couldn't do that until My death and resurrection. This prayer is a guideline.

Father, I praise You and worship You. I thank You for all of my blessings. In Jesus' name Amen.

DAY 7 - SUMMARY
Read Matthew 6:9-14

You need to realize that repeating this prayer mindlessly every night won't do you any good. If you pray it from your heart and realize you are speaking to Me, I will receive your prayer. It is to get you started in prayer.

I want to talk with you. Have a conversation with you, not just have you repeat a prayer mindlessly to make you feel good thinking you are doing your religious duty.

Prayer is communicating with Me so you can get to know Me as we commune together and draw closer to each other. Prayer is a privilege not a religious activity. Prayer is dialogue not monologue. Take time to listen as you pray and I will speak to you.

Father, help me to always pray from my heart and love You with all my heart. In Jesus' name Amen.

NOTES:

&ampampampampampampampampampampampampampampampampampampampampampampampamp

WEEK 31
❖PRAISE AND THANKSGIVING❖

&ampampampampampampampampampampampampampampampampampampampampampampampamp

DAY 1
Read Psalm 100

Make a joyful noise to Me your Lord. Some may be saying, "I can't sing." To Me, it doesn't matter. If you worship from your heart to Me, it is a joyful sound. If you can shout at other public events, such as sports or concerts, surely you can give loud and enthusiastic praise to Me when you are with My people or even in your quiet time.

The Psalms refer to singing more than 70 times so if you have trouble with words to praise and worship Me, find it in the Psalms. This Psalm we are covering this week is a great Psalm to use to worship Me.

Father, I will make a joyful noise to You. I love You and praise You. You are a good, good Father. In Jesus' name Amen.

DAY 2
Read Psalm 100

It's interesting that the word worship in the New Living Translation and serve in the Amplified Translation mean the same thing. You are to serve or worship Me with joy, delight and happiness.

If you don't serve Me with joy and enthusism for the abundant benefits you have received, you will serve your enemies whom I will send against you (Deuteronomy 28:47).

Father, I worship You and serve You with joy and happiness. I love You. In Jesus' name Amen.

DAY 3
Read Psalm 100

      If you are serving Me by participating in a ministry, you are worshipping Me. Do this with joy and delight. Come before My presence with singing.

      I enjoy hearing you sing and make a joyful noise, worshipping Me with all your heart. I am waiting and listening for you.

Father, I find it interesting that to serve You in some capacity in my church or other ministry is worshipping You. I do this with joy and delight. I love You Lord and praise You. In Jesus' name Amen.

DAY 4
Read Psalm 100

      You are to know, acknowledge, and recognize that I am God. I have made you. You are My people and the sheep of My pasture. You are my masterpiece.

      I have created you anew in My image, so you can do the good things I planned for you long ago (Ephesians 2:10). You are My masterpiece, a work of art. Workmanship and masterpiece mean the same thing.

Father, I declare that I acknowledge You and know You are God. I am Yours and the sheep of Your pasture. I am Your masterpiece, a work of art, created in Your image. In Jesus' name Amen.

❧❧❧❧❧❧❧❧❧❧❧

DAY 5
Read Psalm 100

Enter My gates with thanksgiving. Come to Me with thanksgiving, adoration, and praise (Psalm 95:2).

You are to lift your hands in thanks to Me when you are praising Me (Read Psalm 134:2; I Timothy 2:8). Lifting your hands to Me is an act of surrendering as you are praising Me.

Father, I declare I will enter Your gates with thanksgiving and enter Your courts with praise and give thanks to You and praise Your name with uplifted hands. In Jesus' name Amen.

DAY 6
Read Psalm 100

You are to praise Me because of these three things in verse 5.
1. For I am good. I am so good to you. My blessings abound to you in abundance.
2. My mercy and loving kindness are everlasting. I love you so much that I came to die for you so you could live and have fellowship with Me. (Read Psalm 136:1).
3. My faithfulness and truth endure to all generations. I am faithful to My promises.

Father, I declare You are a good, good Father and You love me and Your faithfulness endures forever. In Jesus' name Amen.

DAY 7 - SUMMARY
Read Psalm 100

You are to make a joyful noise to Me, your Lord. You are to serve and worship Me with gladness, delight and happiness. Know and acknowledge Me as God. I made you. You are My masterpiece, a work of art and you are Mine.

Enter My gates and My presence with thanksgiving and affectionately praise My name for I am a good, good Father. I love you unconditionally and I am faithful to My promises forever.

Father, I shout for joy to You. I love You and worship You. I delight in serving You. I am a work of art, a masterpiece. I enter into Your presence with thanksgiving and praise. In Jesus' name Amen.

NOTES:

ක්කක්කක්කක්කක්කක්කක්කක්කක්කක්කක්ක

WEEK 32
❖CHOOSE LIFE❖

කක්කක්කක්කක්කක්කක්කක්කක්කක්කක්ක

DAY 1
Read Deuteronomy 30:19-20; Deuteronomy 28

I give you a choice between life and death. What does this mean? I will bless you if you obey Me. As believers, I have redeemed you from the curse (Galatians 3:13) by My death on the cross but you still need to obey Me because you will reap what you sow (Galatians 6:7-9).

I gave Adam and Eve a choice not to eat the tree of knowledge of good and evil (Genesis. 2:16) but they disobeyed and were banned from the garden to protect them from eating the tree of life. They chose death. Choose Life. I am the truth and the life.

Father, I declare I will choose life by obeying You. In Jesus name Amen.

කක්කක්කක්කක්ක

DAY 2
Read Deuteronomy 30:19-20; Deuteronomy 28

I gave Adam and Eve dominion over all the earth but when they ate of the tree, they gave that dominion over to Satan and their spirit was no longer alive to Me. It was death in the spiritual realm immediately even though they lived physically 900 some years (Genesis 3).

I defeated the devil when I died on the cross and rose from the grave. The devil is still the prince of the air but through My death and resurrection, I have given you authority and power over the devil. The devil can only get to you by you allowing him in. I have given you everything you need for life and godliness (2 Peter 1:3).

Thank You, Father, for the death and resurrection of Jesus. I choose You, Jesus, to be Lord of my life and take the authority You have given me over the devil and walk in victory. In Jesus' name Amen.

DAY 3
Read Deuteronomy 30:19-20; Deuteronomy 28

The adversary the devil walks about like a roaring lion seeking whom he may devour. Submit to Me, resist the devil and he will flee from you (1 Peter 5:8-9). I am not allowing some tragedy in your life, an accident or sickness or job loss to teach you something or humble you.

You don't have to learn from hard knocks. I want to teach you from My Word and the leading of My Spirit (2 Timothy 3:16-17). I will work everything out for your good if you're living for Me (Romans 8:26).

Father, I declare I am meditating on Your Word to receive reproof, correction, and instruction in righteousness. In Jesus' name Amen.

DAY 4
Read Deuteronomy 30:19-20; Deuteronomy 28

You need to know My will from My Word. It is My will that you be healthy. By My stripes you are healed and made whole (Isaiah 53). You need to believe and receive healing the same as you received salvation. I have already provided healing and salvation; you just need to know how to receive it.

Most people when they get sick, they pray and beg Me to heal them. They are waiting on Me. I am waiting on you because I have done it all, provided it all on the cross. You have to resist the devil; sickness is from the devil (Acts 10:38) and I give you the authority to resist the devil in My name (Jesus).

If you are sick in your body, I have not allowed it, you have. Most people don't like to hear that but the devil is a liar and can deceive you if you are not alert to his schemes or you believe the traditions of man and the things that have been taught about healing instead of receiving the truth of My Word.

Father, I declare I know it is Your will to heal me. I will resist the devil and he has to flee from me. My body is God's property and I give you notice, devil, you can't trespass on God's property. In Jesus' name Amen.

DAY 5
Read Deuteronomy 30:19-20; Deuteronomy 28

I am sovereign but I have sovereignly given you a choice. I don't force anything on you. I am a gentleman and love you more than anyone can imagine.

My Word is your instruction manual and you need to study and meditate in it daily so you can choose life and live abundantly.

Father, I know You are a Sovereign God but You give me a choice which is Christ Jesus. I choose life that I and my descendants may live. In Jesus' name Amen.

DAY 6
Read Deuteronomy 30:19-20; Deuteronomy 28

You can make the right choice by loving Me, obeying Me, and committing yourself firmly to Me. This is the key to your life.

The key: love Me and obey Me. If you do that you will live long on the earth. Choose life! Choose Me!

Father, I declare I love You and obey You and commit my life to You. In Jesus' name Amen.

DAY 7 - SUMMARY
Read Deuteronomy 30:19-20; Deuteronomy 28

I give you a choice of life or death and I say to choose life. Realize you will reap what you sow. I give you the authority to resist the devil when bad things happen and be led by My Holy Spirit.

If you are sick, it is not Me allowing this in your life to teach you something but you have allowed it because you don't realize My will for you is healing but you have to receive by faith and take authority over the devil and not wait on Me to heal you. I have already provided healing and I am waiting on You. The same as salvation, you have to believe and receive it. I have already provided it.

I love you and want you to have victory in your life. I have set up laws such as gravity in the natural and spiritual laws that I can't go against. Yes, you will have troubles in life because you are still living on earth and will be affected by things in the earth but I have overcome the earth (John 16:33) and you have My Holy Spirit in your heart to guide you. Listen to Him.

Father, I pray those reading this will receive Your truths and have the faith to act on them. In Jesus' name Amen.

NOTES:

WEEK 33
❖BLESS THE LORD❖
༄༄༄༄༄༄༄༄༄༄༄༄༄༄༄༄༄༄༄༄༄༄༄༄

DAY 1
Read Psalm 103:1-5

You need to bless, affectionately, gratefully praise, salute, congratulate, thank, and kneel down to Me with all of your heart and all that you are.

Read all of Psalm 103 and use different translations as you study My Word.

Father, I praise You Lord with all that I am and with all of my heart. You are worthy of all praise. In Jesus' name Amen.

༄༄༄༄༄༄༄༄༄༄༄
DAY 2
Read Psalm 103:1-5

You are not to forget My benefits. If you bless Me with your whole heart, you will receive benefits from Me. There are four benefits in this passage.

The first one is that I forgive all your iniquities (sins). I died on the cross to save you from your sins, past, present and future sins. I see you, My child, through the blood of Jesus. I see you righteous even though you fail. I want you to be righteousness conscious, not sin conscious.

When I bring things to your attention that aren't right in your life, you can repent and know I am not mad at you. You must stay in fellowship with Me, never run from Me. I am always for you, not against you.

Father, I repent of all the things that are not of You in my life. Thank You for Your love and forgiveness and righteousness. In Jesus' name Amen.

DAY 3
Read Psalm 103:1-5

The second benefit is that I heal all your diseases, cure, repair, mend and restore you to health. The word *rophe,* "one who heals," is the Hebrew word for doctor. The main idea of the verb *rapha'* is physical healing.

You cannot explain away healing because this verse says differently. Scripture states, "I am Yahweh your Physician." I am the God that heals you.

Father, I thank You that You are Yahweh, my Physician. You are the God that heals me. In Jesus' name Amen.

DAY 4
Read Psalm 103:1-5

Notice in verse 3 that it says that I heal <u>all</u> your diseases, not just some but <u>all</u> diseases. Since healing was provided in the Old Testament under the old Covenant you are assured healing is provided in the New Covenant.

Healing was provided in the atonement when I died on the cross (Read Isaiah 53). The first benefit is I forgive all your sins; the second benefit is I heal <u>all</u> your diseases.

Father, I declare that all my sins are forgiven and all my diseases are healed. Thank You Father. In Jesus' name Amen.

છ્છ્છ્છ્છ્છ્છ્છ્છ્છ્છ

DAY 5
Read Psalm 103:1-5

The third benefit that you should not forget is that I redeem your life from destruction. That is I ransom, redeem, repurchase and set you free.

This is what I did for you on the cross. I paid the ransom for your sins and set you free from the pit and corruption.

I beautify, dignify (honor), and crown you with loving kindness and tender mercy. I love you so much and I want everyone to know that love. Don't doubt My love.

Father, give me a revelation of Your love. Sometimes I forget how much You love me. Thank You for Your love and for sending Jesus that I may live free of sin. In Jesus' name Amen.

છ્છ્છ્છ્છ્છ્છ્છ્છ્છ
DAY 6
Read Psalm 103:1-5

The forth benefit that you should not forget is that I fill your life with good things and your youth is renewed as the eagles. I am a good, good Father and want to give you good things. I give you life abundantly (John 10:10). I will do superabundantly, far over and above all that you dare ask or think (Ephesians 3:20).

Your youth is renewed like the eagles (strong, overcoming, soaring (Read Isaiah 40:31). Praise Me with your whole being and I will renew your youth.

Father, I declare You fill my life with good things and renew my youth as the eagles. In Jesus' name Amen.

DAY 7 - SUMMARY
Read Psalm 103:1-5

You are to bless Me with your whole being. Bless Me with all that is within you and don't forget My benefits. There are four benefits from these verses that you should not forget.

They are: 1) I forgive all yours sins 2) I heal <u>all</u> of your diseases 3) I redeem your life from destruction and crown you with lovingkindness and mercy and 4) I fill your life with good things and renew your youth as the eagles. You can be strong, overcoming and soaring above all your problems.

Father, I declare I will not forget that You forgave all my sins, healed all my diseases and sicknesses, redeemed my life from the pit and crowned me with lovingkindness and have mercy on me and will fill my life with good things and renew my youth as the eagle. Thank You Lord. In Jesus' name Amen.

NOTES:

≈≈≈≈≈≈≈≈≈≈≈≈≈≈≈≈≈≈≈≈

WEEK 34
❖WAIT ON THE LORD❖

≈≈≈≈≈≈≈≈≈≈≈≈≈≈≈≈≈≈≈≈

DAY 1
Read Isaiah 40:28-31; Lamentations 3:25-26

You must wait, look for, expect and hope in Me. Jeremiah, even in overwhelming tragedies he experienced; he had hope in My salvation and was willing to wait for it.

Are you willing to wait on Me? It is good that one should hope in and wait quietly for Me.

Father, I declare I will put my hope in You and wait and depend on You for salvation. In Jesus' name Amen.

DAY 2
Read Isaiah 40:28-31; Lamentations 3:25-26

To wait on Me means to go about the routines of life with a fervent, patient hope that I will come back in My time to rule and deal with evil. With this inner attitude it will give you strength to mount up above the moment, with vigor to go on (Read Romans 8:18-30).

Don't ever say, "Under the circumstances" because in Me you can mount up above your circumstances and not be weary.

Father, I declare I will wait on You, trust and depend on You and mount up above my circumstances that try to pull me down and I will not be weary. In Jesus' name Amen.

DAY 3
Read Isaiah 40:28-31; Lamentations 3:25-26

The eagle is a very special bird. I compare you to the eagle. The eagle can go up high and has good eyesight and is able to see small things below. With Me, you are able to be up high above circumstances and I will show you how to overcome them.

The eagle soars above the storms and is able to glide easier along the winds. With Me, you are able to soar above your storms in life. I will enable you to overcome the storms in life.

Father, I declare I will rise above my circumstances and You will enable me to overcome the storms in my life. In Jesus' name Amen.

DAY 4
Read Isaiah 40:28-31; Lamentations 3:25-26

Waiting on Me is important when praying because prayer is dialogue not monologue. It shouldn't be a one-sided conversation. After praying and sending a request to Me, you need to wait on Me to answer.

I am always speaking to you but you must wait and listen for Me to answer. It won't be an audible voice but an inward witness and will sound like you. I will confirm with My Word if you ask Me. I long to fellowship with you. Wait and listen. My Spirit dwells within you and will lead you (1 Corinthians 3:16).

Father, I declare I will wait on You and listen for Your voice. I want to fellowship with You and draw closer to You. In Jesus' name Amen.

DAY 5
Read Isaiah 40:28-31; Lamentations 3:25-26

When you wait on Me and listen for My voice, I will renew your strength and give you power. My strength is power, encouragement sustenance; power to rise or remain firm.

My power gives you the ability to do or act and accomplish what needs to be done. I give you all the strength and power you need to overcome. I give you strength, might and force.

Father, thank You for renewing my strength as the eagle and power to overcome. In Jesus' name Amen.

DAY 6
Read Isaiah 40:28-31; Lamentations 3:25-26

If you wait on Me, you can run and not be weary. I often compare your Christian life to a race (1 Corinthians 9:24; 2 Timothy 4:7; Hebrews 12:1-2) You must keep your eyes on Me and strip away anything that hinders your progress and you won't grow weary.

You also can walk and not faint. I give you the strength and endurance to run and to walk this Christian life. Sometimes you need to slow down in this walk and not get ahead of Me. Wait on Me, run when you need to especially from sins or things that will hinder your walk. Slow down to get the next direction I want to give you. I will renew your strength and you will not grow weary or faint.

Father, I declare I will run this Christian life without anything hindering me and I will walk or slow down to listen for Your voice that is giving me directions. In Jesus' name Amen.

DAY 7 - SUMMARY
Read Isaiah 40:28-31; Lamentations 3:25-26

Those who wait for Me need to look for and hope in Me because as you wait on Me, I will renew your strength and power. You can mount up close to Me as the eagle mounts up close to the sun.

You can run this Christian race and not grow weary. Slow down and walk and listen for Me and you will receive wisdom and direction from Me.

Lord, thank You for renewing my strength as the eagle and giving me strength and power to run this race without becoming weary and tired. I will listen and wait on You. In Jesus' name Amen.

NOTES:

꧁꧂꧁꧂꧁꧂꧁꧂꧁꧂꧁꧂꧁꧂꧁꧂꧁꧂꧁꧂꧁꧂

WEEK 35
❖POWER AT PENTECOST❖

꧁꧂꧁꧂꧁꧂꧁꧂꧁꧂꧁꧂꧁꧂꧁꧂꧁꧂꧁꧂꧁꧂

DAY 1
Read Acts 2:1-4; Matthew 3:11

I told the disciples to go to Jerusalem for the promise of power from on high. They were waiting about ten days after I told them to go to Jerusalem and wait for the promise.

They didn't know what to expect but they went and waited and were in total unity together.

Father, thank You for filling me with the Holy Spirit with the evidence of speaking in tongues which gives me the power to fulfill the mission You have called me to. In Jesus' name Amen.

DAY 2
Read Acts 2:1-4; Matthew 3:11

Some believe that when you accept Me as your Lord and Savior, you receive My Holy Spirit and you do. The filling or baptism of My Spirit is a different experience. I breathed on them and said, "Receive My Holy Spirit" (John 20:22). This is when they were born again and what happens when you accept Me. The disciples were not born again until after I was crucified and rose from the grave and ascended to the Father.

On Pentecost, the work of My Spirit as the Spirit of power (Isaiah 11:2, "might") is to enable the disciples for ministry—witness and service—to fulfill their mission to the world. They are two separate events.

Thank You, Father, for saving me from my sins and filling me with the Holy Spirit with the evidence of speaking in tongues. In Jesus' name Amen.

DAY 3
Read Acts 2:1-4; Matthew 3:11

Verse 4 of Acts 2 is the initial fulfillment of My promise in Acts 1:5 which says "for John truly baptized with water, but you shall be baptized with My Holy Spirit not many days from now."

So the disciples went to Jerusalem and they were all together. They didn't know what to expect but when it came, they would know. Some believer's think they have to wait around to receive but at Pentecost, it was given and you only need to ask and I will fill you. My Spirit isn't going to speak for you. You have to start praising Me and I will give you utterance and enable you to speak in tongues.

Father, I declare I am filled with the Holy Spirit with evidence of speaking in tongues. In Jesus' name Amen.

DAY 4
Read Acts 2:1-4; Matthew 3:11

As they were waiting, suddenly there came a sound as of a rushing mighty wind and it filled the whole house which is the mighty but unseen power of My Holy Spirit (John 3:8). The sound brought the people out to find out what was going on.

What looked like tongues of fire appeared and settled on each one of them which is a fulfillment of what John the Baptist in Matthew 3:11-12 foretold how My Spirit baptism would be accompanied by wind and fire.

Father, You do things suddenly sometimes so let me be prepared and focused on You so I can receive Your "suddenlies." In Jesus' name Amen.

DAY 5
Read Acts 2:1-4; Matthew 3:11

To experience My Holy Spirit fullness you must come to Me. When you come to Me, I will save you, then want to fill you continually, pouring My Holy Spirit upon you, enabling you to declare and demonstrate My living power wherever you go until I come again (Ephesians 5:18).

Father, I come to You and ask You to baptize me with the Holy Spirit continually and give me the utterance of speaking in tongues. In Jesus' name Amen.

DAY 6
Read Acts 2:1-4; Matthew 3:11

They were all filled (diffused throughout their souls) with My Holy Spirit and began to speak in other (different, foreign) languages (tongues). This was the beginning of the Church and I intended it for all generations.

You don't have to be fearful of speaking in tongues. Some say, "I want to know what I am saying". It involves faith in Me. I will give you the interpretation if you ask Me.

The devil wants you to be fearful because he knows when you pray in tongues, you are speaking directly to My Holy Spirit and he doesn't know what you are saying. Trust Me and be filled.

Father, I declare that I am diffused throughout my soul with the Holy Spirit and will speak in tongues as You give me the utterance. In Jesus' name Amen.

DAY 7 - SUMMARY
Read Acts 2:1-4; Matthew 3:11

The truth of My Word must prevail. I desire all My children to receive this separate infilling of My Spirit. This gift will give you power, edification and a way to pray without the interference from the devil. Pray about this gift and seek My opinion. Refuse man's opinion.

I want you to have all that I provide but the devil has deceived many in this and therefore, many Christians don't experience My presence and power like I desire.

Father, give Your people wisdom and understanding regarding being baptized in the Holy Spirit and speaking in tongues. I rebuke all fear and deception. In Jesus' name Amen.

NOTES:

೪೪೪೪೪೪೪೪೪೪೪೪೪೪೪೪೪೪೪೪೪೪೪೪೪

WEEK 36
❖PRIVATE VS PUBLIC TONGUES❖

೪೪೪೪೪೪೪೪೪೪೪೪೪೪೪೪೪೪೪೪೪೪೪೪೪

DAY 1
Read 1 Corinthians 14:1-5; Jude 1:20
John 14-16

When you are speaking in an unknown tongue you are not speaking to men but to Me. It is the perfect prayer and only I know what you are saying unless you ask Me for the interpretation and I will give it to you.

The purpose of praying in tongues is for you to be empowered in ministry that is above the limits of human ability and deeper intimacy for fellowship with Me. The language of worship, intercession, personal edification and revelation from Me are benefits for you when you regularly involve yourself with My Holy Spirit-enabled language as a vital part of your devotional life with Me.

It doesn't give you a superior relationship with Me by praying in tongues. You are no better than the person who does not pray in tongues.

Father, I declare as I pray in the Spirit I will edify myself and receive revelation from You. In Jesus' name Amen.

೪೪೪೪೪೪೪೪೪೪೪

DAY 2
Read 1 Corinthians 14:1-5; Jude1:20
John 14-16

A person who speaks in tongues is strengthened personally, but one who speaks a word of prophecy strengthens the entire church. Speaking in tongues in a Church service must have an interpretation. It is a gift of My Spirit (1 Corinthians 12:10). I want to stress the importance of praying in My Spirit in your prayer and devotional times, not the public tongues and interpretation.

You can pray in the Spirit as you worship at Church because you can run out of words to express your love for Me but that would be between you and Me, not to the Church.

Father, I declare as I pray in the Spirit I edify and strengthen myself and receive revelation from You Lord. In Jesus' name Amen.

DAY 3
Read 1 Corinthians 14:1-5; Jude 1:20
John 14-16

      Praying in My Spirit is your spirit praying to My Spirit. There may be times My Spirit will encourage you to pray for a certain thing or person but you don't know what to pray. Pray in My Spirit and My Spirit knows what is needed as you pray in tongues (Romans 8:26).

      My Spirit does not pray instead of you but My Spirit takes part with you and makes your weak prayers effective. My Spirit intercedes on your behalf before the throne of our Father God (1 John 2:1).

Father, I declare I am available to You to intercede for whoever or whatever You place in my spirit. Your Spirit will cause my prayers to be effective. In Jesus' name Amen.

DAY 4
Read 1 Corinthians 14:1-5; Jude 1:20
John 14-16

      As you pray in tongues, My Spirit will reveal mysteries and secrets. I will tell you things to come and guide you into all truth (John 16:13).

      You don't need to read horoscopes or go to a psychic for I will give you understanding and revelation of My Word as you read and meditate on it. Pray in My Spirit continually and you will be blessed.

Father, I declare You tell me things to come and guide me into all truth and give me revelation of Your Word. In Jesus' name Amen.

꒰꒱꒰꒱꒰꒱꒰꒱꒰꒱꒰꒱

DAY 5
Read 1 Corinthians 14:1-5; Jude 1:20
John 14-16

      I asked our Father that He would give you another Comforter (Counselor, Helper, Intercessor, Advocate, Strengthener and Standby) who would remain with you forever (John 14:16) and live with you constantly and be in you (John 14:17) after My death and resurrection.

      My Holy Spirit lives in you (1 Corinthians 3:16). My Spirit is special and wants you to speak to Him in tongues. He will intercede what is spoken to Me and I will take it to our Father. We are a three part being Father, Son and Holy Spirit. We all work together for your benefit.

Father, I thank You for sending Jesus. Jesus, I thank You for the Holy Spirit. Holy Spirit, I thank You for the baptism of the Holy Spirit with the evidence of speaking in tongues. In Jesus' name Amen.

DAY 6
Read 1 Corinthians 14:1-5; Jude 1:20
John 14-16

      Speaking in tongues charges your spirit like a battery charger charges a battery. It gives strength to your body and power within you. There are many benefits of praying in tongues. Don't let the devil talk you out of it or put fear in you. Ask Me to fill you and I will and you will feel the river bubble up in you. Certain syllables will come to mind and you just need to speak them out.

      Practice praying in tongues daily as much as you can and out of your heart will flow rivers of living water (John 7:38). Don't be drunk with wine but ever be filled *and* stimulated with My Spirit (Ephesians 5:18). Being filled with My Spirit is a continual filling. It is not a one-time event.

Father, I declare I will not fear speaking in tongues. I ask You, Father to fill me to overflowing with evidence of praying in tongues. In Jesus' name Amen.

DAY 7 - SUMMARY
Read 1 Corinthians 14:1-5; Jude1:20
John 14-16

In 1 Corinthians 14:5 Paul says, "I wish you could all speak in tongues…" My wish is the same because it is something you need. You need to be edified, strengthened and helped with your prayers. Being baptized in My Spirit and praying in tongues will do that for you. It also draws you closer to Me. My presence and My peace shall be in you and upon you.

Pray in My Spirit as much as you can and you will receive understanding and revelation of My Word and wisdom for direction in your life.

Father, thank You for filling me with the Holy Spirit and giving me the ability to pray in tongues. In Jesus' name Amen.

NOTES:

❧❧❧❧❧❧❧❧❧❧❧❧❧❧❧❧❧❧❧❧❧❧❧

WEEK 37
❖RIVER OF LIVING WATER❖

❧❧❧❧❧❧❧❧❧❧❧❧❧❧❧❧❧❧❧❧❧❧❧

DAY 1
Read Ezekiel 47:1-12; John 7:37-39

I am going to compare the river in Ezekiel to My Spirit and your life as a believer from the beginning when you accepted Me as your Lord and Savior. Before you were born again it was like being on the shore of this river. You were lost, broken and without hope. You made the decision to live for Me and stepped into this river. When you were first born again you were ankle deep in spiritual things.

It takes a while to grow in Me and My Word but if you stay in My Word and in fellowship with other believers, you will grow. You received My Spirit when you were born again but not baptized in My Spirit yet with evidence of speaking in tongues. That is a separate experience.

Father, I declare I will continue to grow in You and Your Word as I meditate on Your Word. In Jesus' name Amen.

❧❧❧❧❧❧❧❧❧❧❧

DAY 2
Read Ezekiel 47:1-12; John 7:37-39

As you continue on this spiritual journey in the river, you are now knee deep in spiritual things. You are starting to read My Word more and are in a Bible study. There is so much you don't understand but desire to know more.

Keep in fellowship with other believers and stay in My Word. You need to find a time to be with Me. Talk to Me as a friend and you will receive blessings.

Father, I declare I am knee deep in my growing in You and desire to go deeper. In Jesus' name Amen.

DAY 3
Read Ezekiel 47:1-12; John 7:37-39

As you continue on you are now waist deep in spiritual things. You've learned so much but are hungry for so much more. You read in My Word that I am love and love you more than you can even imagine.

It's hard for you to realize how much I love you especially with everything that is going on in your life, the hurts and the sicknesses, all the bad things that seem to be happening. I am for you not against you. My love dwells within you as well as My healing power. It was given to you on the cross the same as salvation. Never doubt My love for you.

Father, I thank You for Your love for me. I declare Your love dwells in me and You are for me and not against me. In Jesus' name Amen.

DAY 4
Read Ezekiel 47:1-12; John 7:37-39

As you continue on this journey, you feel spiritual things are way too deep for you but discovered the baptism of My Spirit with evidence of speaking in tongues. You jumped in the river because it was too deep to continue walking in and feel so alive and overjoyed with My presence.

The more you pray in My Spirit, the more powerful you feel and stirred up in your spirit. As you continue in My Word, revelation and understanding starts coming to you and you are becoming freer in Me.

Father, I declare I pray in the Spirit and receive revelation and understanding and edification in my spirit. Thank You Lord. In Jesus' name Amen.

DAY 5
Read Ezekiel 47:1-12; John 7:37-39

As you flow in this river, you start bearing fruit and receive healing. You feel nothing can keep you down. As you read My Word, you discover you have authority in My name against the devil and his schemes. You realize you don't have to put up with the bad that the devil tries to dish out and that he can only get to you if you allow him.

It's the same with sickness, it is from the devil. You discovered it is My will to heal. The devil comes to steal, kill and destroy. I come to give you life abundantly (John 10:10).

Father, I declare I am bearing fruit for Your kingdom and I am healed. I have power and authority over the devil in Your name. In Jesus' name Amen.

DAY 6
Read Ezekiel 47:1-12; John 7:37-39

Praying in My Spirit is like a bubbling spring flowing out of you which illustrates the difference between your new birth and your experience of the overflowing fullness of the Spirit-filled life. You have become a channel of spiritual refreshment for others.

You notice the difference from when you were first born again and now that you are baptized in My Spirit with evidence of praying in tongues. Continue in your prayer language and continue in My Word and fellowship with other believers. You will be like a tree on the sides of this river that will not wither, turn brown or die and it continues to bear fruit. You will continue to bear fruit and will become a powerful intercessor.

Father, I am so excited to be filled with the Spirit and praying in tongues. I feel stirred up and bubbling over with Your love and power. Thank You for the baptism of the Holy Spirit and praying in tongues. In Jesus' name Amen.

DAY 7 - SUMMARY
Read Ezekiel 47:1-12; John 7:37-39

I want you to flow in My river of living water. Don't stay ankle deep, knee deep or waist deep. Jump in the river of My Spirit and receive life, healing, fruit, understanding and revelation and much more.

Praying in My Spirit is the only way to pray without hindrance from the evil one because he doesn't know what you are praying but I do and I will answer. You will be so full of Me and so stirred up in your spirit as you continue on this spiritual journey. I will lead and guide you where you need to go. Never doubt My love for you. You will never falter if you stay in My Spirit. You will overcome by My blood and the word of your testimony (Revelation 12:11). Confess My Word and proclaim My love for all.

Father, I declare I am flowing in Your river of life. I have jumped in and receive life, healing, fruit and revelation. I pray in the Spirit continually and I am led by Your Spirit. In Jesus' name Amen.

NOTES:

∂∂∂∂∂∂∂∂∂∂∂∂∂∂∂∂∂∂∂∂∂∂∂∂∂∂

WEEK 38
❖SEEK HIS FACE❖

∂∂∂∂∂∂∂∂∂∂∂∂∂∂∂∂∂∂∂∂∂∂∂∂∂∂

DAY 1
Read Psalm 27:8; 1 Chronicles 16:27
Exodus 33:19; John 14:27

When it says in My Word to seek My face it means My presence. Some may be asking, "What does My presence entail? How can you seek My face, My presence, when you can't actually see Me?" You can't see My face with your natural eyes but you can see Me with your spiritual eyes. What do you see when you seek My face, My presence?

The first thing you see is the light of My glory, My honor and majesty. What is the light of My glory? My glory is My goodness.

Father, I see Your face, Your glory, Your presence. Thank You, Lord, for Your glory. In Jesus' name Amen.

DAY 2
Read Psalm 27:8; 1 Chronicles 16:27
Exodus 33:19; John 14:27

Adam and Eve were crowned with glory and honor. When My presence departed, Adam became naked. He lost My glory and honor. They didn't notice their nakedness before the fall because they were covered with My glory and made in My image (Genesis 1:26-28).

I have again crowned you with glory and honor through My death and resurrection. As believer's, you are clothed with My glory and My glory also dwells within you.

Father, thank You for clothing me with glory and honor and for dwelling within me. In Jesus' name Amen.

DAY 3
Read Psalm 27:8; 1 Chronicles 16:27
Exodus 33:19; John 14:27

My strength is My might which is superior power and inflexibility to temptation. I am unmovable, incapable of giving into temptation and I give this to you as you seek Me. My strength is also within you.

Temptation is not sin but if you give into it that is the sin. With My strength, you can overcome any temptation that comes your way. Continue to seek My face and you will have victory.

Father, I declare as I seek You, I receive Your strength, superior power and inability to give in to temptation. Thank You, Lord. In Jesus' name Amen.

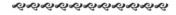

DAY 4
Read Psalm 27:8; 1 Chronicles 16:27
Exodus 33:19; John 14:27

As you seek My face, My presence you will receive My peace.
My peace is rest, quietness, and calmness; an absence of strife; tranquility. I am the Prince of Peace and I give peace to those who call upon Me.

My peace is not as the world gives. You can live this life without letting your hearts be troubled and afraid because as you seek My face, I give you My peace. My peace passes all understanding but you will receive it and you will know it. It is a fruit of My Spirit and dwells within you (Galatians 5:22).

Father, I declare as I seek Your face, I will receive Your peace and I will walk in peace. In Jesus' name Amen.

❧❧❧❧❧❧❧❧❧❧❧❧

DAY 5
Read Psalm 27:8; 1 Chronicles 16:27
Exodus 33:19; John 14:27

As you seek My face, you will see My love because I am love (1 John 4:8). I don't just have love, I am love. It is what I am. I want you to know this love.

If you get the revelation of how much I love you, it will change your attitude and you will experience My blessings. When you see My face, you will see the love in My eyes and you will melt in My presence. My love can be overwhelming because it is hard sometimes for you to think someone could love you as much as I do. I died on the cross for you that you can live. Receive my love. I want to lavish My love on you.

Father, Your love for me is hard to comprehend but I receive it and want to walk in Your love and lavish it on others. Thank You for loving me. In Jesus' name Amen.

❧❧❧❧❧❧❧❧❧❧❧❧

DAY 6
Read Psalm 27:8; 1 Chronicles 16:27
Exodus 33:19; John 14:27

As you seek My face, you will receive all that you need because I AM. I AM whatever you need.

Do you need healing? I AM your healer. Do you need provision? I AM your provider. Do you need peace? I AM your peace. Do you need protection? I AM your refuge and protector and strength. Do you need comfort? I AM your comforter. Whatever you need, I AM.

Seek My face, My presence and find all that you need and desire.

Father, I thank You for being all that I need and desire. I seek Your face, Your presence. In Jesus' name Amen.

የየየየየየየየየ

DAY 7 - SUMMARY
Read Psalm 27:8; 1 Chronicles 16:27
Exodus 33:19; John 14:27

As you seek My face, you will receive the light of My glory. You will receive My strength as you seek My face. You will receive My peace that passes all understanding. Most of all, you will see My love. I will lavish My love on you. Never doubt My love. I give it to you abundantly.

I AM all you need. I AM. Whatever you need and desire I AM. I will never leave you or forsake you. Seek My face and I will always be there for you.

Father, I declare that as I seek Your face, I will see Your glory, Your strength, Your peace, Your abounding love, Your comfort, Your healing power. All that I need I will find in Your presence. In Jesus' name Amen.

NOTES:

એએએએએએએએએએએએએએએએએએએએએએએ

WEEK 39
❖ACKNOWLEDGE HIM❖

એએએએએએએએએએએએએએએએએએએએએએએ

DAY 1
Read Proverbs 3:5-8

You need to lean on, trust in and be confident in Me with everything. Do you lean on, depend on and trust in Me? Sometimes you do and sometimes you don't.

I want you to completely depend on Me. I will hold you up in any situation. You can completely trust and rely on Me. Be confident and have assurance in Me. I am always there for you.

Father, I declare I will lean on, trust in and be confident in You about anything and everything. I can depend on You. In Jesus' name Amen.

એએએએએએએએએએએએ

DAY 2
Read Proverbs 3:5-8

You are to lean on, trust in and be confident in Me with all of your heart and mind which means with your total being, every part of you surrendered to Me as a living sacrifice (Romans 12:1).

Empty yourself completely to allow My Spirit that dwells within you to flow. Keep your mind focused on Me and My Word and you will be victorious in life.

Father, I declare I will lean on, trust in and be confident in You with all my heart and mind, my total being surrendered to You. In Jesus' name Amen.

DAY 3
Read Proverbs 3:5-8

Do not rely on your own insight or understanding because My thoughts are not your thoughts, neither are your ways My ways (Isaiah 55:8-9). My ways and thoughts are beyond yours.

It's good to remember that when you are interceding for others. This is where praying in tongues comes in, the perfect prayer especially when you don't know what to pray for a specific situation or person. Ask Me for My insight and revelation and I will give it to you.

Father, I declare I will not rely on my own insight or understanding. I seek Your insight and revelation. In Jesus' name Amen.

DAY 4
Read Proverbs 3:5-8

I know you struggle sometimes with acknowledging Me in all of your ways and decisions. I want you to have such an intimate relationship with Me that you ask Me about decisions you need to make instead of thinking you have it all figured out.

You are not to rely on your own insight and understanding. Acknowledge Me in <u>all</u> your ways. Things would end up much better if you did. I will direct and make plain your path if you would acknowledge Me.

Father, help me to be so close and intimate with You that I acknowledge You in all my ways and decisions and You will direct my path. In Jesus' name Amen.

DAY 5
Read Proverbs 3:5-8

Don't be wise in your own eyes. You need My wisdom which I give liberally to you if you ask Me (James 1:5).

My wisdom isn't intellectual knowledge but spiritual understanding. My wisdom is insight and revelation, spiritual implication of My Word and My direction about situations you are involved in. Ask Me and you will receive.

Father, I declare I will not be wise in my own eyes but I ask You for Your wisdom and direction. In Jesus' name Amen.

DAY 6
Read Proverbs 3:5-8

You are to reverently fear and worship Me. This fear does not mean to be afraid of Me but to reverence Me, stand in awe of Me. To reverently fear and worship Me is the beginning of wisdom. You are to turn entirely away from evil.

If you acknowledge Me in <u>all</u> your ways, lean on and trust Me and don't be wise in your own eyes but reverently fear and worship Me, it shall be health to your flesh or body and strength to your bones. Do you need healing in your body? You must lean on and trust Me, don't rely on your own understanding, don't be wise in your own eyes, reverently fear Me and turn away from evil and you will be healed.

Father, I worship You and stand in awe of You. As I do, thank You for healing me. In Jesus' name Amen.

DAY 7 - SUMMARY
Read Proverbs 3:5-8

There are six things in these verses you need to do: 1) Lean on, trust in Me with all your heart and mind 2) Do not rely on your own insight or understanding 3) In <u>all</u> your ways acknowledge Me 4) Don't be wise in your own eyes 5) Reverently fear and worship Me and 6) Turn away from evil.

When you do these things, I will direct and make straight and smooth your paths and I will give health to your body and strength to your bones.

Father, I declare I will do these six things and I declare I will receive direction from You and health to my body and strength for my bones. In Jesus' name Amen.

NOTES:

ഏഏഏഏഏഏഏഏഏഏഏഏഏഏഏഏഏഏഏ

WEEK 40
❖PRAY FOR ALL PEOPLE❖

ഏഏഏഏഏഏഏഏഏഏഏഏഏഏഏഏഏഏഏ

DAY 1
Read 1 Timothy 2:1-4

I know you are thinking how can I possibly pray for all men? That is where praying in My Spirit (tongues) comes in. My Spirit knows who and what needs prayer and when you pray in tongues, it is your spirit together with My Holy Spirit praying the perfect prayer.

Father, I declare I will offer up petitions on behalf of all men being led by the Holy Spirit. In Jesus' name Amen.

DAY 2
Read 1 Timothy 2:1-4

Intercede for all people and give thanks for them. Intercession would be pleading another's case, standing in the gap. You can give thanks in your known language and pray intense prayers for a specific person who is dealing with a specific thing which is standing in the gap but also continue praying in My Spirit because you don't know all that a person needs in prayer but My Spirit knows.

Father, I declare I will stand in the gap and intercede for all or for the specific person the Holy Spirit leads me to intercede for. In Jesus' name Amen.

DAY 3
Read 1 Timothy 2:1-4

Prayers offered on behalf of all men would be any and all types of prayers. Give thanksgiving to Me for all men. Pray for the lost and laborers to be sent out.

To pray for all people, you must walk in My love and have My compassion or you won't care about praying for others.

Father, I declare I will pray whatever for whomever You place on my heart and I will also pray in the Spirit as You lead me. In Jesus' name Amen.

DAY 4
Read 1 Timothy 2:1-4

You are also to pray for Kings and all who are in authority. That would include Governmental authority such as the President of the United States or Vice President and all the people involved with them. The state authorities such as Governor and Senators and all involved with them. Local authorities such as Mayor, police, firemen, EMT and all involved with them.

Whether you like who is in these positions or not, you are to pray for them. Pray in the Spirit daily for them.

Father, I pray for Government officials, State officials, and local officials daily as the Holy Spirit leads me. In Jesus' name Amen.

DAY 5
Read 1 Timothy 2:1-4

You say you don't like the President of the United States or your Governor, etc. but to lead a quiet and peaceable life, in all godliness and reverence you need to pray for all those in authority over you.

You need to also pray for your church leaders and your pastor, the shepherd over your church. Pray in My Spirit over all those in authority. It will only take a little of your time to pray and intercede as My Spirit leads you.

Father, I desire a quiet and peaceable life so I will pray and intercede for those in authority over me. In Jesus' name Amen.

DAY 6
Read 1 Timothy 2:1-4

Why do you need to pray for all those in authority over you? Because this kind of praying is good and right and pleasing to Me. If you want to please Me, you must pray and intercede for all those in authority over you. Also, you must pray in faith for it is impossible to please Me without faith (Hebrews 11:6).

I also wish for all men to be saved and able to perceive divine truth. They cannot be saved without you praying. It sounds so easy but it takes time to listen for My voice and to be led by My Spirit in what and who to pray for. So pray in My Spirit as you are led.

Father, I declare I will please You by praying and interceding for all men and for those in authority over me. I pray for the lost because I want none to perish either. In Jesus' name Amen.

DAY 7 - SUMMARY
Read 1 Timothy 2:1-4

You must pray and intercede for all people and for all those in authority over you. When you do, you will have a quiet and peaceable life. This kind of praying pleases Me.

I also want none to perish so you must pray for the lost. You are My representative on the earth to proclaim the truth to the lost and to pray for them. Pray in My Spirit for all people and for those who are lost. I will lead and guide you in your prayers.

Father, I want to please You and have a quiet and peaceable life by praying for all men and praying for those in authority over me. In Jesus' name Amen.

NOTES:

&ed;&ed;&ed;&ed;&ed;&ed;&ed;&ed;&ed;&ed;&ed;&ed;&ed;&ed;&ed;&ed;&ed;&ed;&ed;&ed;&ed;&ed;

WEEK 41
❖SPIRIT OF WISDOM & REVELATION❖

&ed;&ed;&ed;&ed;&ed;&ed;&ed;&ed;&ed;&ed;&ed;&ed;&ed;&ed;&ed;&ed;&ed;&ed;&ed;&ed;&ed;&ed;

DAY 1
Read Ephesians 1:17-18

First of all, Paul says that he always prays to our God, the Father of glory. You are praying to Father God through Me, Jesus. I am your mediator, your intercessor (Hebrews 9:15-24; Romans 8:34).

I stand in the gap for you to our Father which is why you are to pray in My name. I am the only way to our Father. You can freely pray to our Father through Me, Jesus.

Thank You, Father, for Jesus my mediator and intercessor who is always standing in the gap for me. In Jesus' name Amen.

&ed;&ed;&ed;&ed;&ed;&ed;&ed;&ed;&ed;&ed;&ed;

DAY 2
Read Ephesians 1:17-18

Paul is asking our Father to grant the Ephesian Christians a spirit of wisdom and revelation. This wisdom is practical wisdom, extensive insight into the true nature of things. You can ask Me for wisdom and I will give it to you liberally (James 1:5).

Paul is also asking for a revelation (of insight and mysteries in the deep and intimate knowledge of Me.) You need to know Me intimately by knowing My Word and what it says about our Father, Me and My Holy Spirit.

Father, I declare I have a spirit of wisdom and revelation in the knowledge of You. I want to know You more and go deeper in my knowledge of You and draw intimately closer to You. In Jesus' name Amen.

DAY 3
Read Ephesians 1:17-18

I want you to have the eyes of your heart flooded with light so that you can know My wisdom and revelation and knowledge of Me. I will shine upon you and give light to your path.

I AM light and life. If you follow Me, you will no longer be in darkness. In Me, you will no longer be blinded by Satan who blinds unbeliever's minds to the truth.

Father, I declare the eyes of my heart are flooded with Your light and I am no longer blinded by the devil. In Jesus' name Amen.

DAY 4
Read Ephesians 1:17-18

The eyes of your heart are to be enlightened so you can know and understand the hope which I have called you. The hope is My promise and plan that I have called you to. I have a purpose for you. Do you realize Psalm 139:16 says, "You saw me before I was born. Every day of my life was recorded in your book. Every moment was laid out before a single day had passed"? I wrote in a book your life and purposes in heaven before you were born. You need to seek Me and find out what I have written about your life and what I have planned for you.

Another verse says, "For I know the thoughts *and* plans that I have for you, says the Lord, thoughts *and* plans for welfare *and* peace and not for evil, to give you hope in your final outcome (Jeremiah 29:11). Now you know why I say I know the thoughts and plans I have for you. They were written in a book in heaven before you were born.

Father, I declare I know the hope (promise) of Your calling and will follow Your plan for my life. In Jesus' name Amen.

DAY 5
Read Ephesians 1:17-18

What is My glorious inheritance? This is where you need to study My Word to find out what you have in Me and who you are in Me.

You are adopted by our Father God (Romans 8:15). He is Your Father and you are His child and you have all that I, Jesus have. All that you have inherited is glorious and from God our Father.

Father, I declare You are my Father and I am Your child because You adopted me. I have inherited all that Jesus inherits and it is glorious. Thank You Lord. In Jesus' name Amen.

DAY 6
Read Ephesians 1:17-18

You will know how rich My glorious inheritance is in the saints. Saints are My set-apart ones. Did you know you are a saint? (1 Corinthians 1:2). If you call on Me and accept Me as your Lord and Savior, you are a saint. All believers have been set-apart to belong to Me and placed in Me and you are to continuously grow in holiness.

You are sanctified (set-apart) in Me, holy as I am holy. What are you set-apart from? You are set-apart from this world. You are not to conform to this world but be transformed by the renewing of your mind by My Word (Romans 12:2).

Father, I declare I am Your child so, therefore, I am a sanctified, set-apart saint, holy as You are holy in Christ. In Jesus' name Amen.

DAY 7 - SUMMARY
Read Ephesians 1:17-18

      This is a prayer Paul prayed for the Church in Ephesus. These prayers are good to pray for yourself or for others. It is directly from My Word so you know I will honor these prayers.

      In this prayer, Paul is asking Me to grant them a spirit of wisdom and revelation in the knowledge of Me. You need to know Me intimately. You can know Me by the eyes of your heart being enlightened and also know and understand the hope (promise) I have called you to and the rich inheritance I have given you with all My set-apart ones. I have a plan for everyone which I wrote in a book in heaven before you were born.

Father, I declare I have a spirit of wisdom and revelation to know You more intimately. The eyes of my heart are enlightened and I have an understanding of the plans which You have called me to and written in a book in heaven before I was born. I declare I have a glorious inheritance along with all His set-apart ones. Thank You Lord. In Jesus' name Amen.

NOTES:

WEEK 42
❖GREATNESS OF HIS POWER❖

DAY 1
Read Ephesians 1:19-23

This prayer started out with Paul asking Me to grant them a spirit of wisdom and revelation in the knowledge of Me and that the eyes of their heart be enlightened so they can understand the hope I have called them and to know My glorious inheritance

You know the immeasurable, unlimited and surpassing greatness of My power in and for you. Did you catch that? My immeasurable, unlimited and surpassing greatness of My power is in you and for you. It is in you. My power, dominion and reigning authority and majesty are in you. I live in you. There is so much of Me available to you. If you would realize all that I have provided, you would be a power house.

Father, I declare Your power and authority is in me and for me and I have the victory in my life. In Jesus' name Amen.

DAY 2
Read Ephesians 1:19-23

My power is working in and through you. I demonstrated this power when I was raised from the dead. The same power that raised Me from the dead dwells within you, flowing through your veins, sending healing throughout your body. I know you may be thinking, if that is the case, why do you still have problems or sickness, etc.? Because you have to know that My power is there and that by faith you have to activate it, just as you had to accept and activate your faith to accept My salvation.

I have provided everything you need. I am waiting on you. Most people are waiting on Me to do something but I have done it all and it is all available to you by faith.

Father, I declare Your power is in me and I walk in faith to activate it in my life in every situation. I declare by the stripes You bore on Your body I am healed and made whole. You took my pain and bore my sicknesses on the cross. In Jesus' name Amen.

DAY 3
Read Ephesians 1:19-23

I am seated at our Father's right hand in heavenly places. You are also raised up together (giving you joint seating with Me) in the heavenly realm (Ephesians 2:6). I grant that you share in the present work of My kingdom's power.

I am sitting at the right hand of our Father God to signify that My work is finished. I said on the cross, "It is finished." (John 19:30). You being seated with Me signifies you don't have to do anything on your own or in your own effort. It is through Me you have the victory.

Father, I declare I am raised together with Jesus in heavenly places and share in His present work of the kingdom. In Jesus' name Amen.

DAY 4
Read Ephesians 1:19-23

You need spiritual wisdom and understanding so you will know that I am far above all rule, authority, and power and over every name that is named (Philippians 2:9-11).

You need to know what is involved in My name and what you have in Me. To have victory, you need to understand how to use My name in prayer and in spiritual warfare.

Father, I declare I have spiritual wisdom and understanding and the eyes of my heart are enlightened to know that Jesus is far above all rule, authority, and power and over every name that is named. I have the same power in me because Jesus dwells in me. In Jesus' name Amen.

やややややややややや

DAY 5
Read Ephesians 1:19-23

All things are under My feet. All authority (all power of rule) in heaven and on earth has been given to Me (Matthew 28:18). I have given it to you as well because you are in Me.

I am head of the Church which makes you My body. You are one body and parts of one another and dependent on one another and on Me (Romans 12:5).

Father, I declare I have all authority on earth given by Jesus so I can have the victory in Him. In Jesus' name Amen.

やややややややややや

DAY 6
Read Ephesians 1:19-23

You are My body. You are the fullness of Me. I fill all in all and you are complete in Me. I fill everything everywhere with Myself. What does this mean? As My body, you are made complete in Me.

You have all power and authority in you and wherever you go, I go with you. You are carriers of My Holy Spirit. You represent Me in this world. It's like the wind, it blows (breathes) where it wills; and though you hear its sound yet you neither know where it comes from nor where it is going. So it is with everyone born of My Spirit (John 3:8). You can't see the wind but you can feel it and see the effects of it. You can't see My Spirit but you can feel My presence and see the effects of My Spirit.

I fill everything everywhere with Myself. My Spirit is in everything everywhere including each one of you.

Father, I declare that I am complete in Christ and that I am the fullness of Him. I have all power and authority of Christ in me. I am a carrier of His Spirit. He fills me and fills everything everywhere with Himself. In Jesus' name Amen.

DAY 7 - SUMMARY
Read Ephesians 1:19-23

Paul prayed this prayer for the Christian Ephesians. You can pray this prayer for yourselves and for others as Paul did and I will answer this prayer.

Paul prayed for a spirit of wisdom and revelation in the knowledge of Me by having the eyes of your heart enlightened so that you can know: 1) and understand the hope and purpose I have called you to. 2) How rich your inheritance is. 3) What is the immeasurable and unlimited greatness of My power that is in you and for you. 4) The power which I demonstrated when I rose from the dead and that this power is in you. 5) Father God seated Me at His right hand in the heavenly realm and you are seated with Me. 6) I am seated far above all rule and authority and power and dominion. 7) My name is above all names. 8) All things are under My feet. 9) I am the supreme head of the Church and you are My body. 10) In that body lives the full measure of Me and makes everything complete and fills everything everywhere with Myself.

Father, I pray for a spirit of wisdom and revelation knowledge of You by having the eyes of my heart enlightened so I can know and understand the hope and purpose You have called me to. To know Your rich inheritance, the greatness of Your power that is in me, so that I can know that You are seated in the heavenly realm and I am seated with You. Your name is above all names and all things are under Your feet. You are the head and I am Your body and I have the fullness of You in me. In Jesus' name Amen.

NOTES:

∂∂∂∂∂∂∂∂∂∂∂∂∂∂∂∂∂∂∂∂∂∂∂∂∂∂

WEEK 43
❖SPIRITUAL GROWTH❖

∂∂∂∂∂∂∂∂∂∂∂∂∂∂∂∂∂∂∂∂∂∂∂∂∂∂

DAY 1
Read Ephesians 3:16-21

This is Paul's second letter to the Ephesian Church. Paul prayed that from My glorious, unlimited resources I will empower you with inner strength through My Spirit. My glorious resources are unlimited so you can come to Me and receive all you need no matter how big or little your concern may be.

Do you need inner strength today? I will empower you with inner strength by My Holy Spirit. I indwell your innermost being and personality. You are the temple of My Holy Spirit (1 Corinthians 3:16).

Father, I declare I receive from Your glorious unlimited resources strength in my innermost being because You dwell in me. In Jesus' name Amen.

∂∂∂∂∂∂∂∂∂∂∂∂

DAY 2
Read Ephesians 3:16-21

It is through your faith that I dwell and abide in your heart as Lord. If you accepted Me as your Lord and Savior, My Spirit dwells within you. I have made My permanent home in you.

My love dwells in you and you can be rooted deep in My love and secure in My love. I am love and I love you more than you can imagine but I want you to grasp (get ahold) of My love and experience it.

Father, I declare I have the faith that You abide in my heart as Lord. I am rooted and founded securely on Your love and experience that love daily. In Jesus' name Amen.

DAY 3
Read Ephesians 3:16-21

I want you to experience My love what is the breadth (wide to reach the world and beyond) the length (stretches from eternity to eternity) high (can raise anyone to heavenly places in Me) and depth (deep enough to rescue people from sin and the grip of Satan).

Come to know this love through experience for yourself, personally and have My love reproduced in you. You are to love as I love and through Me, it is possible because I am love and dwell in you.

Father, I declare I experience Your love how wide, long, high, and deep that love is. I declare I know You and Your love personally. Thank You Lord. In Jesus' name Amen.

DAY 4
Read Ephesians 3:16-21

This love surpasses mere knowledge. You cannot experience it intellectually just in your mind but by faith and knowing Me personally and intimately. The more you know of My love, there is always more because My love is inexhaustible. By experiencing My love, you can be filled (through all your being) to all the fullness and power that comes from Me. You can become a body wholly filled and flooded with Me (Colossians 2:10). Get this revelation so you can be empowered by Me and have victory in your life.

I am a gentleman and I have made My love, power, and authority and every promise and My presence available to you but if you don't know that it will not manifest fully in your life. I am waiting on you to do your part in receiving all I have provided and activate by faith in your life.

Father, I want to know You and Your love more and walk in the fullness of You and be wholly filled and flooded with You. I declare I am a power house for You. In Jesus' name Amen.

જ્જ્જ્જ્જ્જ્જ્જ્જ્જ્જ્

DAY 5
Read Ephesians 3:16-21

My power is working within you and is able to carry out My purpose in and through you by faith. I will do superabundantly far over and above all that you dare ask or think beyond your highest prayers, desires, thoughts, hopes and dreams. It's according to the power that is working in you by faith. It is impossible to ask Me for too much. I want to give you an abundant life (John 10:10).

My thoughts and ways are higher than your thoughts and ways (Isaiah 55:8-9) so what you ask, think, desire, hope or dream, I will do superabundantly far over and above those things. Seek My thoughts and My ways and you will be blessed.

Father, I declare that Your power works within me according to my faith and You are able to do superabundantly, far over and above all I ask, think, desire, hope or dream. Thank You, Lord for Your goodness. In Jesus' name Amen.

DAY 6
Read Ephesians 3:16-21

My glory is in you because I dwell in you. My glory is My main attribute. You are My masterpiece of grace for you are My body, I am the head and it is by My grace and My mercy that you are filled and walk in My glory.

Father, I declare Your glory is in the Church and in Christ Jesus. I give You all glory and honor. Your glory dwells within me and by faith, I walk in that glory. In Jesus' name Amen.

DAY 7 - SUMMARY
Read Ephesians 3:16-21

This is such a powerful prayer that you can pray for yourself or others and I will answer this prayer. Paul is asking that you be strengthened with mighty power in the inner man by My Holy Spirit. I dwell within you and make My permanent home in you.

Be rooted deep and secure in My love. Grasp what is the breadth, length, height and depth of that love and come to know My love by personally knowing Me. I love you so much and want you to bask in that love. Be filled to the fullness of Me and be filled and flooded with Me. I permeate your whole being. According to the power and your faith working in you, I will carry out My purpose and do superabundantly above all that you think, desire, dream and hope for.

My glory is in the Church and in Me; therefore, it is in you. Walk in My love and glory and have victory in your life.

Father, I declare I am strengthened and You dwell in me. I am rooted and secure in Your love. I am filled with the fullness of Christ and flooded with Your presence. Thank You for doing superabundantly more than I ask for. I give You all glory and honor. In Jesus' name Amen.

NOTES:

WEEK 44
❖LET LOVE OVERFLOW❖

DAY 1
Read Philippians 1:9-11

This prayer Paul prayed for the Philippian Christians. He's praying that their love will overflow and excel. This love He is talking about is My love (agape love). It says in Romans 5:5 that My love has been poured out in your heart because My Holy Spirit lives in your heart. So you shouldn't say you can't love a certain person because My love is in you. I am love so the agape love is in you.

What is agape love? It is My unconditional love. You need to show the same love for others and you have no excuse because agape love lives in you.

Father, I declare Your love is poured out in my heart. Therefore, I walk in love. In Jesus' name Amen.

DAY 2
Read Philippians 1:9-11

I want you to understand what really matters. My love gave you the ability to both discern and choose what is morally best so that you may live pure and blameless lives until I return.

You can be unaffected by the evil in this world by renewing your mind to My Word and you will be blameless and guiltless because you walk in My Spirit and My love, not in the flesh.

Father, I understand and discern what really matters and choose what is morally best so I can live pure and blameless in You. Thank You, Lord. In Jesus' name Amen.

DAY 3
Read Philippians 1:9-11

My love is patient and kind. I am not jealous, boastful or proud. I am not rude and I do not demand My own way. I am not irritable and I do not keep a record of being wronged. I do not rejoice in injustice but rejoice when truth prevails. I will never give up or lose faith. I am always hopeful and endure through every circumstance. I never fail (1 Corinthians 13:4-7).

This is My love and it dwells within you. I know you are thinking there is no way you can love everyone this way. If you are walking in My Spirit, you can walk in this love. If you are walking in the flesh, it will be impossible to love others this way.

Father, I declare I am patient and kind. I am not jealous, boastful or proud. I am not rude and I do not demand my own way. I am not irritable and I do not keep a record of being wronged. I do not rejoice in injustice but rejoice when truth prevails. I will never give up or lose faith. I am always hopeful and endure through every circumstance. I never fail. In Jesus' name Amen.

DAY 4
Read Philippians 1:9-11

I want you always to be filled with the fruit of your salvation. John 15:4 says you must remain or abide in the vine because you cannot bear fruit unless you abide in Me. A branch that is severed from the vine cannot produce fruit.

To remain in Me is to die to your flesh and walk in My Spirit. Seek My presence, meditate on My Word, be obedient to My Word and you will produce fruit.

Father, I declare I walk in the Spirit and abide in You and Your Word. I produce fruit. In Jesus' name Amen.

DAY 5
Read Philippians 1:9-11

What is the fruit of your salvation? Righteous character produced by Me. Galatians 5 22-23 lists the fruit of the Spirit. They are love, joy, peace, patience, kindness, goodness, faithfulness, gentleness, and self-control. If you accepted Me as your Lord and Savior, you have this fruit in you. Remember, My Spirit dwells in you and I have provided all you need for godliness. Ask My Spirit to manifest this fruit in your life and He will.

Just knowing you have this fruit in you makes a difference. If you had a million dollars in your bank account but didn't know it, it wouldn't benefit you. It is the same with knowing what you have in Me.

Father, I declare I walk in the fruit of the Spirit which is love, joy, peace, patience, kindness, goodness, faithfulness, gentleness, and self-control. In Jesus' name Amen.

DAY 6
Read Philippians 1:9-11

Righteousness is being right with Me, being conformed to My revealed will in all respects. 1 Corinthians 1:30 says "I made you right with our Father God; I made you pure and holy and I freed you from sin".

I hear a lot of Christians say, "I am a sinner saved by grace." That is not true according to 1 Corinthians 1:30. Sure, you are still going to sin and mess up but as long as you repent (1 John 1:9) you are forgiven and righteous before Me. Father God sees you through My blood and says you are righteous. You can boldly come to His throne into His presence (Hebrews 4:16).

Become righteousness conscious rather than sin conscious. When you are thinking always that you are a sinner, you don't feel worthy to come into My presence. That is why I died for you so that you are worthy and righteous through My blood to come into our Father God's presence.

Thank You, Father, for sending Jesus to take my sins and cause me to be righteous (in right standing) with You. I declare I am free from sin and come boldly to Your throne. In Jesus' name Amen.

DAY 7 - SUMMARY
Read Philippians 1:9-11

Paul prays that your love will overflow more and more. My love (agape love) lives in you so you have no excuse not to love as I love. 1 Corinthians 13 gives what My love entails. You can walk in this love.

I want you to understand what really matters which is that by your love you will live pure and blameless lives until I return.

You are to be filled with the fruit of salvation which is listed in Galatians 5:22-23. Walk in the Spirit and this fruit will manifest in your life. It is within you.

Righteous character in your life is produced by Me. Righteousness is right standing with Me. Our Father God sees you through My shed blood. He sees you righteous, not as a sinner. Come boldly to His throne.

Father, I pray that my love will overflow more and more. I will grow in knowledge and understanding. My love will give me the ability to live pure and blameless until Jesus returns. May I always be filled with the fruit of salvation. I will walk in Your righteousness because of Jesus and bring glory and praise to God. Thank You, Jesus. In Jesus' name Amen.

NOTES:

~~~~~~

WEEK 45
❖STRENGTHENED WITH POWER❖

~~~~~~

DAY 1
Read Colossians 1:9-11

Paul is asking Me to give the Colossian Church complete knowledge of My will and Spiritual wisdom which is intelligently assessing a situation. Spiritual wisdom is My wisdom, not the wisdom of the world. What is My will? One thing that is My will for you is to be thankful in all circumstances, always be joyful and never stop praying.

The second thing is to not copy the behavior and customs of this world, but let Me transform you into a new person by the way you think. Then you will learn to know My will for you, which is good and pleasing and perfect (Romans 12:2).

Father, I declare I have complete knowledge of Your will and spiritual wisdom and understanding. I will be thankful in all circumstances and be joyful and never stop praying. Your will is good, pleasing and perfect. In Jesus' name Amen.

~~~~~~~~~~~~~~~

DAY 2
Read Colossians 1:9-11

I will strengthen and enable you with My glorious power so you will have all the endurance and patience you need. I know sometimes you struggle with patience. Don't struggle. Patience is a fruit of My Spirit and I am willing to give it to you. Remember, it is in you because My Spirit lives in you. Believe and you shall see it manifest in your life.

Don't believe the myth that asking for patience brings trials into your life. I will enable and strengthen you to have patience. By asking, I do not cause pain and trials in your life to give you patience. Just by being in the world, you will have trials and tribulation but I have overcome the world (John 16:33).

Father, I declare I am strengthened and enabled by You with Your glorious power to have all the endurance and patience I need to have victory in my life. In Jesus' name Amen.

DAY 3
Read Colossians 1:9-11

By having the complete knowledge of My will and spiritual wisdom and understanding your life will always honor and please Me and your life will produce every kind of good fruit. I talk about the fruit of My Spirit in Galatians 5:22-23. Check it out.

What honors and pleases Me? Your thoughts and attitude need to be renewed by My Spirit (Ephesians 4:23) and put on the new nature I have given you and be renewed and become like Me (Colossians 3:10).

When you accept Me as Lord and Savior, you become a new creation in your spirit, old things are passed away and everything becomes new but your mind and flesh does not change. You still need to renew your mind to My Word, die to your flesh nature and let My Holy Spirit guide you and take over. You must be obedient to My Word and the leading of My Spirit. You must walk in faith. You cannot please Me without faith.

Father, I declare the way I live honors and pleases You and I produce good fruit. I walk in the Spirit not the flesh and I walk by faith. In Jesus' name Amen.

DAY 4
Read Colossians 1:9-11

You are filled with joy. It is also a fruit of My Spirit and dwells within you. Joy is not an emotion you have because of outward things in your life. It comes from within you; it comes from My Spirit within you.

Even in the midst of trials, you can be joyful because My Spirit will empower you to be joyful. You can endure and have patience with joy. The joy I give you is your strength. As you become aware of My Holy Spirit fruit in you, it will manifest in your life.

Father, I declare I walk in Your Spirit and the fruit of the Spirit manifests in my life so I can have patience and endurance with joy. In Jesus' name Amen.

DAY 5
Read Colossians 1:9-11

Always come to Me with a grateful heart being thankful in all circumstances (I Thessalonians 5:18), for this is My will for you. I know it is sometimes hard to be thankful when you are going through a tough time but be thankful that I am with you and I will bring you through every trial you face.

Do not fear because fear is not from Me. I have given you love, power and a sound mind (2 Timothy 1:7).

Father, I declare I have a grateful heart no matter what trial I face in life because You are with me and give me love, power and a sound mind and You enable me to be victorious in every situation. In Jesus' name Amen.

DAY 6
Read Colossians 1:9-11

I have enabled and authorized you to share in the inheritance that belongs to you as My child because you live in the light. What is My inheritance? All things that pertain to life and godliness as well as great and precious promises I have given to you through Me (2 Peter 1:3-4).

I desire to bless you and help you through the storms in life. You don't have to struggle as you do. Just seek My face and I'll deliver you and help you through all your struggles and storms in life.

Thank You, Father, for enabling me to share in Your inheritance that belongs to me and Your great and precious promises. In Jesus' name Amen.

DAY 7 - SUMMARY
Read Colossians 1:9-11

As you pray this prayer for yourself and others, I will give you complete knowledge of My will and I will give you My wisdom, not the wisdom of this world. I will give you understanding in which you can assess every situation. I will help you live in the way that honors and pleases Me and produces fruit. As you draw close to Me and know Me better, you will grow and learn My ways.

I will strengthen you with My glorious power so you will have endurance and patience in every trial you may face. I will fill you with My joy and you will receive strength because My joy is your strength. Be thankful always and receive your inheritance that belongs to you as My child and walk in My precious promises.

Father, I declare I have complete knowledge of Your will and You give me Your wisdom and understanding. The way I live honors and pleases You and I produce good fruit. I grow as I draw closer to You and learn more about You. You give me strength to endure and have patience. I have the joy of the Lord which strengthens me. I receive Your inheritance and walk in Your precious promises. In Jesus' name Amen.

NOTES:

WEEK 46
❖ANSWERED PRAYER❖

DAY 1
Read Acts 12:3, 11-16

Do you feel you are in a prison? Peter was physically in prison. He wasn't too worried, he was sleeping when My angel came to wake him up and lead him out of the prison.

You may not be in prison but feel you are a prisoner because of situations in your life. Look to Me, rest in Me, and you will be freed from those things that have you captive. I will open the prison doors and set you free. If you are in prison, I will give you peace in the place you are at. Trust Me and I will give you all you need in that place.

Father, I declare I will look to You and trust You to open the prison doors and set me free from all those things that have me captive. In Jesus' name Amen.

DAY 2
Read Acts 12:3, 11-16

My church was earnestly praying for Peter. That is why I sent My angel to lead Peter out of the prison, because the church was earnestly praying. I heard their prayers. They were fervent and persistent in their prayers and they were together in unity.

They were praying together in faith and agreement. Peter thought it was a vision but after the angel left he realized it was real and went to the house where the congregation was praying. Does your church come together and pray? My church must be a praying church. My body must come together in unity and in prayer for My work to be done. I've called you to prayer. Answer the call.

Father, I declare I will answer Your call to prayer. My church is a praying church and we come together in unity and pray. In Jesus' name Amen.

DAY 3
Read Acts 12:3, 11-16

When you pray, believe what you are praying for and expect Me to answer. Don't doubt and be amazed as this church was when their prayer was answered.

Peter came knocking on the door and the servant girl ran back to tell the people he was there. They didn't believe her. Peter kept knocking until they came back and opened it for him. The servant girl was overjoyed when she heard Peter's voice and went back to tell the others. She should've opened the door and doubt would not have entered their minds.

Father, I declare when I pray I will believe and expect an answer from You. I will not allow doubt to enter into my heart. In Jesus' name Amen.

DAY 4
Read Acts 12:3, 11-16

Why are you so amazed when I answer prayers? Why pray if you don't expect Me to answer? I hear your prayers and answer your prayers but most of you don't expect an answer so you don't receive.

You must pray in faith for Me to answer you. You cannot please Me without faith. Come to Me with faith and expectation and I will answer your prayers. Do not doubt when problems arise, stay in faith and expectation.

Father, I declare I will come to You in faith and in expectation that You will answer my prayers. I will not doubt but will believe You hear my prayers and will answer them as I stay in faith. In Jesus' name Amen.

DAY 5
Read Acts 12:3, 11-16

Do not doubt when you pray. The devil will try to discourage you that I won't answer your prayer but if you do not doubt, I will answer. The devil is a liar and comes to steal, kill and destroy you because you are My child. Doubt causes you to be double-minded and unstable in all your ways (James 1:6-8).

If you are double-minded and doubt you cannot expect to receive anything from Me. So have faith and trust Me when you pray. Believe you will receive what you ask for.

Search My Word for issues you are dealing with and stand on My Word. My Word says I am your God that heals you (Exodus 15:26) so stand on that Word and receive your healing.

Father, I declare I will not doubt and be double-minded when I pray but will ask in faith and believe I receive what I asked for. I stand on Your Word. In Jesus' name Amen.

DAY 6
Read Acts 12:3, 11-16

Show hospitality to strangers because at times you may be entertaining angels without realizing it (Hebrews 13:2). My angels are all around to serve you and protect you (Hebrews 1:14). Just as I sent an angel to lead Peter out of prison, I will send angels to help you. You may not see the angels as Peter did but realize they are all around you.

You need to speak My Word because My angels come to help you by My Word. If you speak My Word about healing, the angels can help you to get healing but if you talk sickness all the time, it causes your angels to come to a standstill.

Speak life not death. Speak My Word not negative things or doubt and your angels can serve you as you need them.

Father, I will show hospitality to strangers because sometimes strangers may be angels to help me and encourage me. I will speak Your Word and not doubt or speak negative things so my angels can serve me according to Your will. In Jesus' name Amen.

DAY 7 - SUMMARY
Read Acts 12:3, 11-16

If you feel you are in a prison because of situations in life, I can set you free. Trust Me and believe you will receive and you can have what you are believing for. I will open those prison doors and set you free.

Come together, Church, in unity and faith. The body of Christ must be in prayer to be able to do My work effectively. As you pray, believe and do not doubt. Do not be double-minded. Pray and speak My Word and I will hear your prayers and answer them.

Don't be amazed when I answer your prayers. Pray with expectancy that I will answer and do not doubt. If you don't expect Me to answer, you will not receive. You must come to Me in faith. Faith is what pleases Me.

Show hospitality to strangers because you may be entertaining angels. My angels are all around you, protecting you and ministering to you. Do not worship angels; they are just there to minister to you what My Word says. Speak My Word and they will help you. Speak doubt and negative things; it will cause them to come to a standstill.

Father, I declare that You have opened the prison doors and have set me free. I trust You and believe I receive when I pray. I pray in unity with others and pray in faith without doubting. I pray with expectancy of my prayers being answered. Thank You for the angels around me. I will speak Your Word so they can minister according to Your will. I will not speak doubt or negative things because I do not want my angels to come to a standstill. In Jesus' name Amen.

NOTES:

෪෪෪෪෪෪෪෪෪෪෪෪෪෪෪෪෪෪෪෪෪෪෪෪

WEEK 47
❖A CONTRAST NOT COMPARISON❖

෪෪෪෪෪෪෪෪෪෪෪෪෪෪෪෪෪෪෪෪෪෪෪෪

DAY 1
Read Luke 11:5-13

Would you consider this person a friend if you came to him in the middle of the night with a need? I wouldn't consider him a friend. Most believers consider Me as this so called friend that they have to beg for help from Me. People seem to trust other people more than they do Me.

I am not like this so called friend. I would never treat My children like this so called friend. I am your friend and I am available to you at any time of need. You don't have to beg me to help you. I am always with you and will never forsake you.

Father, I thank You that You are not like this so called friend in this portion of Scripture but You are a faithful friend that is always there for me and will meet my needs. In Jesus' name Amen.

DAY 2
Read Luke 11:5-13

If a friend wouldn't treat you this badly why do you think I, your Heavenly Father, would treat you this way. This person is a selfish human being and is not a child of mine. This is not godly behavior.

Why do you think I am up in heaven, mad at you, making you beg for what you need? I love you more than you can ever imagine and I want to bless you abundantly. Never doubt My love. I am here for you always.

Father, I declare You are my friend and You love me and bless me abundantly. In Jesus' name Amen.

DAY 3
Read Luke 11:5-13

What is prayer? Is it like this person going to his so called friend and begging to get what he needs? No you don't have to come to Me begging for what you need. Prayer is communion and fellowship with Me. It's coming to Me and saying, "Father, I love You" and hearing Me answer "I love you too". It's listening to Me in your heart and feeling My pleasure as you spend time with Me.

If you did that, you wouldn't have to spend much time asking for things because they would supernaturally show up.

Father, I declare I come to You to fellowship with You and love on You. I know You will take care of all my needs without me begging. You know what I need even before I ask. Thank You. In Jesus' name Amen.

DAY 4
Read Luke 11:5-13

The next couple of verses after these say ask and you will receive, seek and you will find and knock and the door will be opened. You don't have to beg Me. I hear you and I am willing to give to you.

Sometimes, if you are interceding for another person, it may not seem like I am answering your prayers but the other person has a will and choices and they may void the prayer you prayed for them. You cannot claim another person for salvation but you can pray that the blinders that Satan has put on them be removed. If they ignore My conviction, then they voided your prayer so you need to keep on praying for the blinders to be removed and their ears be opened to My voice and silence the voice of the devil. Pray this way until they have accepted salvation.

You must pray in faith and with the right motive for Me to answer your prayers. If you are not receiving, check your faith and your motives.

Father, I declare that when I ask, I receive. When I seek, I will find. When I knock, the door will be opened to me. I have no need to beg You to answer my prayers. In Jesus' name Amen.

DAY 5
Read Luke 11:5-13

This parable goes on in verses 11-13 comparing Me to a father. If a father wouldn't give bad things to their children, how much more will I give the Holy Spirit and anything else you need.

If father's did to their children what most people accuse Me of such as putting sickness on you to teach you something or taking your child from you, or any number of bad things that happen, that person would be turned in for child abuse.

Why do bad things happen? Because you are in a fallen world and I have set up spiritual laws I must abide by. I've given you everything you need to be victorious in this life. Read My Word to find out what those things are and walk in them and you will be victorious.

Father, I declare I read Your Word and walk in obedience to it. As I do, I will have victory in my life. In Jesus' name Amen.

DAY 6
Read Luke 11:5-13

Healing, deliverance, prosperity, and salvation don't "just happen". Spiritual laws must be obeyed in order to receive the desired results. Healing is provided through My blood and the stripes that were put on Me. My Spirit dwells within you so healing, prosperity, deliverance, and My glory dwells in you. Everything I was and have, you have within you. You must learn how to release from the inside out for these things to manifest. I have already given healing to you; you need to confess My Word, speak to the mountain and do not doubt and it will be cast into the sea (Mark 11:23).

These are spiritual laws I have spoken about. I give you the power and authority to cast the mountain into the sea instead of you begging me to remove the mountain. I tell you to submit to Me, resist the devil and he will flee from you (James 4:7). I can't resist him for you. It doesn't work that way. I have given you My power and authority to resist him.

Father, I declare I walk in the power and authority You have given me. I submit to You and resist the devil and he flees from me. In Jesus' name Amen.

DAY 7 - SUMMARY
Read Luke 11:5-13

This parable is a contrast not a comparison to Me. I am not like this so called friend. Sometimes you need to be persistent in your praying because of demonic interference, lack of faith and doubting or the other person voiding your prayer by ignoring the convictions, etc. You do not have to beg Me to answer you. I heard you the first time. I am willing to help and available to you, whenever you come to Me.

Ask and you will receive. Seek and you will find. Knock and the door will be opened to you. You need to do it in faith, not doubting and you will receive. I've given you power and authority to stand your ground against the devil. He can only do what you allow him to do. I told you to submit to Me, resist the devil and he will flee from you. You do that and you will have the victory in your life.

Everything you need dwells in you. I've provided healing, believe you receive and you will have it. I am not withholding anything from you but you must operate according to the spiritual laws set up or you will not receive. I know many people believe because I am God I can do anything but I function according to the laws set up. Gravity is a law and I cannot change it to save someone that is jumping off a building. If I did, everyone else would be in trouble. Read and meditate on My Word and act on the Word and you will receive and be victorious in this life.

Father, I declare I receive when I ask in faith. I meditate on Your Word and I am obedient to it. I submit to You, resist the devil and he will flee from me and I will have victory in my life. Everything I need dwells in me and I will release it from the inside of me to the natural and receive the victory. In Jesus' name Amen.

NOTES:

≈≈≈≈≈≈≈≈≈≈≈≈≈≈≈≈≈≈≈≈≈≈≈≈≈≈≈≈

WEEK 48
❖THE UNJUST JUDGE❖

≈≈≈≈≈≈≈≈≈≈≈≈≈≈≈≈≈≈≈≈≈≈≈≈≈≈≈

DAY 1
Read Luke 18:1-8

This is another parable like last week which is a contrast not a comparison to Me. Most people think I am like this unjust judge but I am nothing like him. You should always pray and never give up but remember, you must pray in faith and not doubt.

Sometimes the holdup is because of demonic hindrance like in Daniel 10 where Daniel prayed for 21 days but I heard and answered his prayer immediately but the devil blocked My angel coming to give Daniel the answer until reinforcement angels came to help him. So don't give up. You do not have to beg Me to answer your prayers. Just stand your ground, confess My Word over the situation and stay in faith.

Father, I declare You are not like this unjust judge. You hear my prayers and answer immediately. I will stand my ground, confess Your Word and stay in faith. In Jesus' name Amen.

DAY 2
Read Luke 18:1-8

This judge was more worried about the woman wearing him out and his reputation than the woman. He was selfish and thought only of himself. I am a God of love and will not treat you this way. I hear your prayers; even know what you need before you even ask.

When you read My Word, don't take what you read out of context. Read the whole passage. People stop at verse 5 thinking I am that unjust judge. Go on to read the rest of the story before you judge.

Father, I declare You are not like this unjust judge but a loving and just God. You hear my prayers and care about me. In Jesus' name Amen.

DAY 3
Read Luke 18:1-8

Even the unjust judge gave justice because she was wearing him out and he rendered a just decision in the end. So don't you think I will surely give justice to My chosen people who cry out to Me day and night? I will not keep putting you off as this unjust judge did.

Who are My chosen people? My chosen people are those who are born again, possessed by Me, living and walking by My Spirit.

Father, I declare You are just and hear my prayers. You will not put me off. I am Your chosen child, living and walking by Your Spirit. In Jesus' name Amen.

DAY 4
Read Luke 18:1-8

I will grant justice to you quickly. It may not seem quick to you but remember, your thoughts are not My thoughts, your ways are not My ways. Stay in faith and never give up and you will have the victory.

Remember, you don't have to beg Me for anything. I hear you and I will answer quickly.

Father, I declare You will grant justice quickly. I must stay in faith and never give up. In Jesus' name Amen.

DAY 5
Read Luke 18:1-8

When I return, how many will I find on the earth that have faith. It is impossible to please Me without faith. You must believe that I exist and that I reward those who seek Me (Hebrews 11:6).

What is faith? Faith is the confidence of what you hope for will actually happen; it is assurance of things you cannot see.

I have given you a measure of faith and you must develop and grow your faith by the Word of God. That measure of faith is the same for all.

Father, I have faith in You and believe that You exist and reward me because I seek You. I study and meditate on Your Word so I can grow and develop my faith. In Jesus' name Amen.

DAY 6
Read Luke 18:1-8

Faith comes by hearing and hearing My Word. It is important to be in My Word daily, meditating on it, not just reading it. Listen to the Word preached by those you can trust to preach My uncompromised Word.

When you pray, you must have faith. Have My kind of faith (Mark 11:22). You have to have faith to speak to your mountains, do not doubt and believe what you say and you will receive what you have asked for.

I am for you, not against you and hear your prayers. I will answer quickly but you must have faith.

Father, I declare I have Your kind of faith. I develop my faith by hearing and meditating on Your Word. I will speak to my mountains and they will move because I do not doubt but believe what I say and will receive what I ask for. In Jesus' name Amen.

DAY 7 - SUMMARY
Read Luke 18:1-8

This parable is a contrast not a comparison to Me. I am not like this unjust judge. I will render to you quickly what you need. You must have faith and not doubt.

Sometimes you need to be persistent because of the demonic hindrances and need to stand your ground against them. You don't need to come to Me and beg for things. I heard your cries and requests and will answer quickly. My thoughts and ways are not your thoughts and ways so have faith and do not doubt. I am for you not against you. I love you and care about all your needs and desires.

Father, I thank You that you will come quickly to me when I call to You. You hear my prayers and as I walk in faith and not doubt, I will receive what I believe for. I love You Lord. In Jesus' name Amen.

NOTES:

WEEK 49
❖TO KNOW HIM❖

DAY 1
Read Philippians 3:1-11

Your primary pursuit in life as a believer should be to want to know Me and experience the mighty power that raised Me from the dead.

What do I mean to know Me? Know My ways, know My Word, know what I have provided as a believer and who you are in Me. Seek My face and enjoy My presence. Consider everything else as garbage compared to knowing Me and being obedient to My will. You will have life abundantly bestowed on you.

Father, I declare I want to know You and experience the mighty power that raised Jesus from the dead. I want to know Your ways, Your Word, Your thoughts and who I am and what I have as a believer. As I do, I will have an abundant life. In Jesus' name Amen.

DAY 2
Read Philippians 3:1-11

To know Me is to encounter Me. When you come to Me you are open to the Spirit who gives the freedom of unveiled access to Me (2 Corinthians 3:16). You can see and reflect My glory.

Pursue knowing Me and communing with Me as My character engulfs you with this glory and holy wonder because I passionately desire intimate friendship with you.

Father, I want to encounter You and have unveiled access to You and see Your glory and reflect Your glory. I want to commune with You and also desire an intimate friendship with You. In Jesus' name Amen.

DAY 3
Read Philippians 3:1-11

In Exodus 33:18, Moses asked Me to show him My glory which is stated as My goodness. I wouldn't allow him to see My face but I placed him in the cleft of the rock, placed My hand over him, passed by him and allowed him to see My back.

Today, in Me, I have given you access into My presence. You can see all My glory and enjoy My presence but only through Me. When I come back for all of you, then you will see My face. If you know Me, you know our Father God, because I have revealed Him to you.

Father, thank You for Your glory and Your presence that I can experience through Jesus Christ. I want to know You more. In Jesus' name Amen.

DAY 4
Read Philippians 3:1-11

My faithful love never ends. My mercy will never cease. I am faithful and new mercies begin each day, as you come to Me.

Come into My presence and receive My favor. I am your merciful Father and the God of all comfort (2 Corinthians 1:3). I am so rich in mercy and I love you so much. I gave you life when I was raised from the dead (Ephesians 2:4-5).

Thank You, Father, for Your love and mercy on my life. I come into Your presence and receive Your love and favor. In Jesus' name Amen.

DAY 5
Read Philippians 3:1-11

As long as your heart is turned to Me in childlike trust, I will enable you to complete the work to which I have called you. You will experience My mighty power. It is by My Spirit who enables you to know Me and know My ways. My Holy Spirit is in you and will lead you in the way you should go.

You must stay in communion with Me to know Me and to experience My resurrection power. You are righteous through your faith in Me so always know you can boldly come to Me. I am here for you. Never doubt My love.

Father, my heart is turned to You in childlike trust. I declare You will enable me to complete the work You have called me to and I will experience Your mighty power. I want to know You more and draw closer to You. I will not doubt Your love. In Jesus' name Amen.

DAY 6
Read Philippians 3:1-11

Knowing Me not only means experiencing the power of the My resurrection, but also sharing in My sufferings. What do I mean by this? You are to live godly lives, even in the midst of trials, suffering, or persecution. Circumstances do not affect My godly principles for living.

You will experience persecution if you stand for My godly principles and suffer for My name. If you are suffering sickness or disease, that is the oppression of the devil. That is not suffering for My sake. It is not My will for you to suffer sickness and disease. I've given you My power and authority to come against sickness and disease.

The world did not like Me so the world will not like you. I give the example of how to live My godly principles and how to handle trials and tribulation. You will have trials and tribulation but I have overcome the world (John 16:33) so stay in faith and you will experience the power of My resurrection and peace and victory.

Father, I know I will share in Christ's sufferings as a believer in Him because the world did not like Jesus, the world will not like me. I declare I will stay in faith and experience the power of Jesus' resurrection and have victory in my life. In Jesus' name Amen.

DAY 7 - SUMMARY
Read Philippians 3:1-11

I want you to know Me and experience My mighty power that raised Me from the dead. This power is in you. Learn to release it from the inside out.

To know Me is to encounter Me. I was sent to give you access into My presence. You can boldly come into My presence and experience My glory. I passionately desire you to commune with Me and to have intimate friendship with you.

I love you with an everlasting love. I know it is hard for you to fathom how much I love you. Come into My presence and receive My love and favor.

As long as your heart is turned to Me, I will enable you to complete the work I have called you to. It is by My Spirit that enables you to know Me and My ways. Know that I dwell in you and all you need for life and godliness dwells in you. Stop struggling, know what you have in Me and walk in it.

You will experience persecution in this life for My name but remember in your trials, I have overcome the world. You can overcome by My blood and the word of your testimony and not loving your life but willing to die (Revelation 12:11).

Father, I declare I know You and experience Your mighty power that raised Jesus from the dead. This power is in me and I will release it. I want to have an encounter with You and I seek Your presence. I want to have an intimate friendship with You as well. Thank You for the Holy Spirit that enables me to know You and Your ways. I will stop struggling and walk in the Spirit. I may suffer for the name of Jesus but will overcome by the blood of Jesus and the word of my testimony. I love You Lord. In Jesus' name Amen.

NOTES:

ৡৡৡৡৡৡৡৡৡৡৡৡৡৡৡৡৡৡৡৡৡৡৡ

WEEK 50
❖A NEW CREATURE❖

ৡৡৡৡৡৡৡৡৡৡৡৡৡৡৡৡৡৡৡৡৡৡৡ

DAY 1
Read 2 Corinthians 5:17

If you accepted Me, Jesus Christ, as your Lord and Savior, you are a new creation. You were hoping by this verse that everything would be different in your mind and body, as well as your spirit. The only thing that is brand new is your spirit. Your mind and body has to be renewed by My Word to be changed.

You can be transformed completely by the renewing of your mind by My Word (Romans 12:2). Once you understand who you are in Me and what you have in Me, you will be transformed.

Thank You, Father, for sending Jesus to die for me so that I can be a new creation in Christ. I am renewing my mind to Your Word so that I can be transformed to Your ways. In Jesus' name Amen.

ৡৡৡৡৡৡৡৡৡৡ

DAY 2
Read 2 Corinthians 5:17

Your spirit is brand new. You were living in sin and separated from our Father God before you accepted Me. I came and took your sin and sicknesses and set you free from sin and bondage. I gave My life willingly so that you could come boldly into My presence and commune with Me. Our Father God loved you so much that He sent Me to die for your sins. I took all your sin upon the cross and you are no longer a slave to sin. You are forgiven of all sin.

Through the shedding of My blood, you are now a child of our Father God (Ephesians 1:5) and a joint heir with Me. You have inherited all blessings that I have (Ephesians 1:11). You have everything you need for life and godliness (2 Peter 1:3).

Father, I declare I have accepted Jesus as my Lord and Savior. I am no longer a slave to sin. I can come boldly into Your presence and commune with You. Thank You for forgiving me of all my sins and giving me every spiritual blessing and all I need for life and godliness in Christ. I am Your child and a joint heir with Jesus. In Jesus' name Amen.

DAY 3
Read 2 Corinthians 5:17

  I want you to know what the fresh and new is. There are many, many things I have given to you. There are many promises in My Word that you can claim. Many are conditional to your obedience to My Word and spiritual laws. I cannot mention all My promises or what you have in Me but I am going to mention a few.

  You are righteous in My sight through My blood shed on the cross (2 Corinthians 5:21). Our Father only sees My blood that took your sin. You can boldly come into My presence. Don't be sin conscious anymore thinking of your unworthiness. You are worthy through My blood. I have forgiven you of all your sin. Come believing and confessing that you are righteous in My sight. You are in right standing with Me if you are born again. You are no longer a slave to sin but a slave to righteousness.

Father, I declare I am righteous before You. I am in right standing with You. I will come boldly into Your presence and commune with You. I love You Lord. In Jesus' name Amen.

DAY 4
Read 2 Corinthians 5:17

  You are My temple. My Spirit lives within you and you do not belong to yourself (1 Corinthians 3:16; 6:19). You belong to Me as My beloved child. You have access to the Spirit to lead and guide you in all things.

  Since you are My temple and I live in you, I am always with you wherever you go. I will never leave you or forsake you. Be aware of My Spirit and My presence. You can talk to Me at any time. I will hear you and I will answer you.

Father, I declare I am the temple of the Holy Spirit. I belong to You as Your beloved child. I allow You to lead and guide me in all things. I commune with You and enjoy Your presence. In Jesus' name Amen.

DAY 5
Read 2 Corinthians 5:17

You can do all things through Me because I empower you with strength. You are not weak but strong. The Spirit that raised Me from the dead dwells in you so you have power and strength to do all that I called you to.

My healing power dwells in you. By my stripes you were healed (1 Peter 2:24). Healing was provided on the cross. Through Me I forgave you all your sins and healed all your diseases (Psalm 103:3).

You must believe when you pray and you will receive. Healing is in your spirit, you need to learn how to release it in the natural. Just as you must have faith to receive salvation, you have to have faith for healing to manifest. Don't be moved by what you see or feel, be moved only by what My Word says and you will receive.

Father, I declare I can do all things through Christ who empowers me. Thank You for Your healing power that dwells in me. I believe and I receive what You have provided. In Jesus' name Amen.

DAY 6
Read 2 Corinthians 5:17

You are more than a conqueror through Me and have the victory in this life (Romans 8:37). You may not feel victorious but you are. I have given you all authority and power to overcome all attacks of Satan. You have it all dwelling in you. It's up to you to release it. I will back you up but I've sent you to heal the sick and set the captives free. Don't beg Me to heal. It's in you to be released to others and yourself. Don't say "God get the devil off of me." I've told you to resist the devil and he will flee.

You are My representative on the earth and I've given you all you need to do what I've called you to do. I'm waiting on you to get that revelation and move in My power and authority.

Father, I declare I am more than a conqueror through Christ and have the victory through the power and authority that has been given to me. I am to go and heal the sick and set the captives free as Your representative on this earth. I will walk in the power and authority You have given to me. In Jesus' name Amen.

DAY 7 - SUMMARY
Read 2 Corinthians 5:17

The day you accepted Me as your Lord and Savior you became a new creation in your spirit. The old is passed away, the new has come. Your body and mind hasn't changed but you can be changed by renewing your mind to My Word.

You were a slave to sin but you are now a slave to righteousness. I see you righteous through the blood shed on the cross. You are in right standing with Me. Come boldly into My presence. All your sins are forgiven and all of your diseases are healed through Me.

You can do all things through Me for I empower you. You are not weak but strong. You are My temple that My Spirit lives in. He is always there for you. No matter where you are at or what you are doing, My Spirit is there for you.

You are more than a conqueror through Me. You have all power and authority in you to be victorious in your life. Healing power is within you. You must pray in faith and you shall receive. You are My representative on the earth. I am sending you out as I did the disciples to heal the sick and set the captives free. Everything you need for life and godliness is within you. Walk in My Spirit and you will be able to do all things I did and so much more.

Father, I declare I am a new creation in Christ. I renew my mind to Your Word so that I will be transformed into what You desire me to be on this earth. I am worthy and righteous in Your eyes because of the blood of Jesus. He forgave me of all my sins and healed me of all my diseases. I am more than a conqueror and have all power and authority in me to be victorious over Satan and in this life. Thank You Lord. In Jesus' name Amen.

NOTES:

ન્ક્ર્ન્ક્ર્ન્ક્ર્ન્ક્ર્ન્ક્ર્ન્ક્ર્ન્ક્ર્ન્ક્ર્ન્ક્ર્ન્ક્ર્ન્ક્ર્ન્ક્ર્

WEEK 51
❖ETERNAL LIFE❖

ન્ક્ર્ન્ક્ર્ન્ક્ર્ન્ક્ર્ન્ક્ર્ન્ક્ર્ન્ક્ર્ન્ક્ર્ન્ક્ર્ન્ક્ર્ન્ક્ર્ન્ક્ર્

DAY 1
Read John 17:1-3

When you accepted Me as Lord and Savior, you also received eternal life. This verse is saying that eternal life is to know our Father God and to know Me the anointed One.

You thought eternal life was what you receive when you get to heaven but it is much more than that. Eternal life starts the day you accepted Me. Eternal life is in you now.

Thank You, Father, for eternal life that is in me now because of Jesus Christ. I declare I know You and I know Christ the anointed one. In Jesus' name Amen.

ન્ક્ર્ન્ક્ર્ન્ક્ર્ન્ક્ર્ન્ક્ર્ન્ક્ર્

DAY 2
Read John 17:1-3

I have mentioned several times the importance of knowing Our Father God and knowing Me especially through Paul's prayers (Ephesians 1:17; 3:16-19; Colossians 1:9-14). To know our Father and Me is to have eternal life.

John 1:1, 4 says, "In the beginning [before all time] was the Word (Christ), and the Word was with God, and the Word was God Himself." I was the Word and I was with our Father from the beginning. I am eternal and I am in you so eternal life begins when you accepted Me.

Father, I declare Jesus was the Word and was with You from the beginning. I have eternal life in me now. In Jesus' name Amen.

DAY 3
Read John 17:1-3

What does it mean to have eternal life now rather than when you get to heaven. Remember this verse says eternal life means to know our Father and Me as the anointed One. You must know our Father and Me before you get to heaven.

To pray effectively and to walk victoriously in this life, you must know our Father and His love and to know Me, Jesus, as Lord and Savior. Father has given you eternal life through Me. Whoever has Me has life, if you do not have Me, Jesus, you do not have life (1 John 5:11-12).

Father, I declare I know You and I know Jesus Christ as my Lord and Savior. Therefore, I have eternal life now. In Jesus' name Amen.

DAY 4
Read John 17:1-3

You have eternal life now because, our Father, Jesus, and Holy Spirit dwell in you. The Word (Bible) is eternal. I am the Word from the beginning. I planted eternity in your heart (Ecclesiastes 3:11) and mind and given you purpose.

Come to Me and I will give you understanding and knowledge of who I am. This eternal life is present life of grace and future life of glory.

Father, I declare I come to You and desire to know You more and to know Jesus more. Thank You for Your grace and Your glory. In Jesus' name Amen.

DAY 5
Read John 17:1-3

Believe in Me and you will have eternal life, now in this life and forever (John 3:36). Your spirit is eternal. If you know Me and our Father, you will go to heaven and live forever. If you do not know Me and our Father, you will go to hell and live forever in torment.

If you drink the living water (which is the Spirit) I give, it bubbles up within you and gives you eternal life (John 4:14). Those who listen to My message and believe that our Father sent Me will have eternal life (John 5:24). It is My will that all who believe in Me will have eternal life (John 6:40). My commands lead to eternal life (John 12:50).

Father, I believe in You and that You sent Jesus to die for me. I have been given eternal life through my faith in Jesus and by listening to Your message and obeying Your commands. In Jesus' name Amen.

DAY 6
Read John 17:1-3

I will give eternal life to those who keep on doing good and seeking after My glory, honor and immortality that I offer (Romans 2:7). Eternal life is a free gift from our Father through Me (Romans 6:23). Fight the good fight of faith and hold tightly to the eternal life that I have given you (1Timothy 6:12). I give you abundant life (John 10:10) because I am life and this eternal life is in you.

You have no excuse for not knowing Me. For ever since the world was created, you have seen the earth and sky. Through everything I made, you can clearly see My invisible qualities—My eternal power and divine nature (Romans 1:20).

Father, I declare I have eternal life because I do good and seek Your glory, honor and immortality that you offer. Thank You for the gift of eternal life. I want to know You more and more. In Jesus' name Amen.

DAY 7 - SUMMARY
Read John 17:1-3

Eternal life is to know Our Father and to know Me, the Anointed One, whom our Father sent. Eternal life is more than going to heaven; eternal life is in you now as a child of God.

Eternal life is the Word. I am the Word. Whoever has Me has eternal life. I give you abundant life. Come into our Father's presence and know Him and know Me, Jesus.

You have no excuse for not knowing Me. For ever since the world was created, you have seen the earth and sky. Through everything I made, you can clearly see My invisible qualities, My eternal power and divine nature.

Thank You, Father, for sending Jesus and giving me eternal life. This eternal life dwells in me. I have no excuse for not knowing You because of the world You created and everything You have made. I love You and want to know You more. In Jesus' name Amen.

NOTES:

≈≈≈≈≈≈≈≈≈≈≈≈≈≈≈≈≈≈≈≈≈

WEEK 52
❖GOD'S LOVE❖

≈≈≈≈≈≈≈≈≈≈≈≈≈≈≈≈≈≈≈≈≈

DAY 1
Read Romans 4:25-5:11

My love is in you. I am love (1 John 4:16). I don't just act in love; I am love. I have poured My love in your heart through My Holy Spirit who has been given to you. Perfect love casts out fear. So do not fear.

Father God loves you so much He sent Me, Jesus, to die for your sins so that you could be free from sin and live forever.

I love you so much; it is hard for you to completely comprehend it. I want you to know the depth, height, length and width of My love (Ephesians 3:18) so you can be deeply rooted in My love.

Father, I declare You have poured out Your love in my heart through the Holy Spirit Who was given to me. I want to know the depth, length, height, and width of Your love. In Jesus' name Amen.

Day 2
Read Romans 4:25-5:11

I tell you to love one another but you say you can't love certain people. My love is within you so you can love as I love. I never tell you to do anything that I have not supplied what you need to do it.

My love is poured out in your heart and I will love others through you as you yield your feelings to Me and allow My love to be expressed. My Word tells you how to walk in love and be led by My Spirit. Meditate on it and receive the revelation.

Father, I declare I walk in love and I am led by Your Spirit to love others as You love. Thank You for Your love that is in my heart. In Jesus' name Amen.

DAY 3
Read Romans 4:25-5:11

You seem to have trouble loving Me with all of your heart because you don't think I answer your prayers or you think I make you sick. You lost a friend or loved one and think I allowed it. I answer your prayers and I do not cause bad things to happen in your life. I love you and want good things for you (James 1:17).

I have given you free will and power and authority and spiritual laws have been given that I cannot undo. I have given you all things for life and godliness. I have given My Holy Spirit to you to help you and lead you on the right path.

Walk in My Spirit and walk in My love and you will have victory. If a prayer seems to not be answered, check your faith and your motives (James 4:3). Ask in faith and you shall receive (Mark 11:24).

I declare I love You with all of my heart. All good things come from You. I walk in the Spirit and I walk in love. In Jesus' name Amen.

DAY 4
Read Romans 4:25-5:11

My love is agape love. It is an unconditional love that I have for everyone. The characteristics of My love are in 1 Corinthians 13:4-8. Love is patient and kind. Love is not jealous or boastful or proud or rude. It does not demand its own way. It is not irritable, and it keeps no record of being wronged. It does not rejoice about injustice but rejoices whenever the truth wins out. Love never gives up, never loses faith, is always hopeful and endures through every circumstance…Love will last forever. This love dwells in you.

Father, I declare I have Your love in my heart. I will be patient and kind. I will not be jealous or boastful or proud or rude. I do not demand my own way. I am not irritable, and I do not keep a record of being wronged. I do not rejoice about injustice but rejoice whenever the truth wins out. I never give up, never lose faith, always hopeful and endure through every circumstance. In Jesus' name Amen.

DAY 5
Read Romans 4:25-5:11

Let love be your highest goal! Without love, without Me, you can do nothing and it will mean nothing without love (1 Corinthians 13:1-3). All things must be done in love.

Remember, My love dwells within you. I will help you love the most unlovable person around. I have made it possible for you to love as I love. Have faith to release it to others as you are led by My Spirit.

I will love through you if you will allow Me to. If you yield your life to Me, you will love all those who are lost and need to be loved. You are My representative on the earth. I cannot reach out and hug a person, but you can. Love displayed will make someone's day.

Father, I declare love is my highest goal. If I do anything without love, it is nothing. I will walk in Your love and reach out to those who are lost and need to be loved. We all need to be loved and I declare I am Your representative on the earth to display Your love. In Jesus' name Amen.

DAY 6
Read Romans 4:25-5:11

Continue to love one another for love comes from Me. Anyone who loves is My child and knows Me. But if you do not love you do not know Me because I am love and I dwell in you (1 John 4:1). As you live in Me, your love grows more perfect.

There are many evil and fearful things going on in this world but do not fear because My perfect love casts out fear. I did not give you a spirit of fear but of power, love and a sound mind. Walk in My love and you will not fear. Loving Me means to keep My commandments for My commandments are not burdensome and you will be victorious (1 John 5:4).

Father, I declare I will love others. Because I walk in love, I am Your child and I know You. I will not fear because Your perfect love casts out fear. I have the spirit of power, love and a sound mind. In Jesus' name Amen.

DAY 7-SUMMARY
Read Romans 4:25-5:11

My love is in you. I am love. I poured out My love in your heart by My Holy Spirit Who has been given to you. I love you so much I sent My Son, Jesus to die for you and save you from your sins. I know it is hard for you to comprehend My love but I want you to know My love.

My love is in you to give to others. You are to love one another and through Me you can. I will love others through you as you allow Me to. It is hard for you to love others because you have problems loving Me.

You do not think I love you because prayers don't seem answered or bad things happen in your life but I am here for you and I love you. I answer your prayers. I cannot go against My Spiritual laws that are set up. You must pray in faith and with the right motives. I give you all you need for life and godliness. I give you power and authority to resist evil. You wait on Me to answer when I am waiting on you to walk in faith and take your authority I've given you. Resist the devil and he will flee from you. Ask in faith and you shall receive.

My love is patient and kind. Love is not jealous or boastful or proud or rude. It does not demand its own way. It is not irritable, and it keeps no record of being wronged. It does not rejoice about injustice but rejoices whenever the truth wins out. Love never gives up, never loses faith, is always hopeful and endures through every circumstance…Love will last forever. This love dwells in you. Walk in this love and you will be victorious.

It is very important for you to realize how much I love you. If you don't realize how much I love you, you won't have faith that I will answer your prayers and have your best interest in mind. That is why I ended this book talking about My love. I want it to be fresh on your mind always. I love you!

Thank You, Father, for Your love and that You are love. God is love, love is God. We cannot get away from Your love. It dwells in me and I will manifest it out to those around me. Help me grow closer to You and know this love that abounds in my heart. In Jesus' name Amen.

NOTES:

Prayer for Salvation and Baptism of the Holy Spirit

Heavenly Father, I come to You in the name of Jesus. I know that I am a sinner and have been separated from You. Your Word says whoever shall call upon the name of the Lord [invoking, adoring, and worshiping the Lord—Christ] shall be saved (Acts 2:21 Amplified Bible, Classic Edition). I am calling on You. I pray and ask Jesus to come into my heart and be Lord of my life. I confess that Jesus is Lord, and I believe in my heart that God raised Him from the dead. I repent of sin. I renounce it. I renounce the devil and everything he stands for. Jesus is my Lord.

I am now reborn! I am a Christian—a child of Almighty God! I am also asking You to fill me with the Holy Spirit. Holy Spirit, rise up within me as I praise God. I fully expect to speak with other tongues as You give me the utterance (Acts 2:4). In Jesus' name Amen.

Begin to praise God for filling you with the Holy Spirit. Speak those words and syllables you receive—not in your own language, but the language given to you by the Holy Spirit. You have to use your own voice. God will not force you to speak. Get into a Spirit-filled church and stay in the Word of God.